The Doctrine
of Salvation

The Doctrine of Salvation

A. W. Pink

Baker Book House
Grand Rapids, Michigan

Copyright 1975 by Baker Book House Company
ISBN: 0-8010-6980-7
Library of Congress Catalog Card Number: 75-18228

PHOTOLITHOPRINTED BY CUSHING - MALLOY, INC.
ANN ARBOR, MICHIGAN, UNITED STATES OF AMERICA
1975

Contents

Contents

PART ONE

Regeneration,
or the New Birth

1 Introduction

Two chief obstacles lie in the way of the salvation of any of Adam's fallen descendants: bondage to the guilt and penalty of sin, bondage to the power and presence of sin; or, in other words, their being bound for hell and their being unfit for heaven. These obstacles are, so far as man is concerned, entirely insurmountable. This fact was unequivocally established by Christ, when, in answer to His disciples' question, "Who then can be saved?" He answered, "With men this is *impossible.*" A lost sinner might more easily create a world than save his own soul. But (forever be His name praised), the Lord Jesus went on to say, "With *God* all things *are* possible" (Matt. 19:25-26). Yes, problems which completely baffle human wisdom are solvable by Omniscience; tasks which defy the utmost efforts of man, are easily accomplished by Omnipotence. Nowhere is this fact more strikingly exemplified than in God's saving of the sinner.

As intimated above, two things are absolutely essential in order to salvation: deliverance from the guilt and penalty of sin, deliverance from the power and presence of sin. The one is secured by the mediatorial work of Christ; the other is accomplished by the effectual operations of the Holy Spirit. The one is the blessed result of what the Lord Jesus did *for* God's people; the other is the glorious consequence of what the Holy Spirit does *in* God's people. The one takes place when, having been brought to lie in the dust as an empty-handed beggar, faith is enabled to lay hold of Christ— God now justifies from all things, and the trembling, penitent, but believing sinner receives a free and full pardon. The other takes place gradually, in distinct stages, under the divine blessings of regeneration, sanctification, and glorification. In regeneration, indwelling sin receives its death-wound, though not its death. In sanctification, the regenerated soul is shown the sink of corruption that dwells within, and is taught to loathe and hate himself. At glorification both soul and body will be forever delivered from every vestige and effect of sin.

Now a vital and saving knowledge of these divine truths cannot be acquired by a mere study of them. No amount of pouring over the Scriptures, no painstaking examination of the soundest doctrinal treatises, no exercise of the intellect, is able to secure the slightest spiritual insight into them. True, the diligent seeker may attain a natural knowledge, an intellectual apprehension of them, just as one born blind may obtain a notional knowledge of the colorings of the flowers or the beauties of a sunset; but the natural man can no more arrive at a *spiritual knowledge* of spiritual things than a blind man can a true knowledge of natural things—yea, than a man in his grave can know what is going on in the world he has left. Nor can anything short of divine power bring the proud heart to a felt realization of this humbling fact; only as God supernaturally enlightens is any soul made conscious of the awful spiritual darkness in which it naturally dwells.

The truth of what has just been said is established by the plain and solemn declaration in I Corinthians 2:14, "But the natural man receiveth not the things of the Spirit of God: for they are foolishness unto him: neither can he know them, because they are spiritually discerned." Alas that so many evade the sharp point of this verse by imagining it applies not to them, mistaking an intellectual assent to spiritual things for an experimental acquaintance of them. An external knowledge of divine truth, as revealed in Scripture, may charm the mind and form ground for speculation and conversation, but unless there is a divine *application* of them to the conscience and heart, such knowledge will be of no more avail in the hour of death than the pleasing images of our dreams are of any satisfaction when we awake. How awful to think that multitudes of professing Christians will awaken in hell to discover that *their* knowledge of divine truth was no more substantial than a dream.

While it be true that no man by searching can find out God (Job 11:7), and that the mysteries of His kingdom are sealed secrets until He deigns to reveal them to the soul (Matt. 13:11), nevertheless, it is also true that God is pleased to use means in the conveyance of heavenly light to our sin-darkened understandings. It is for this reason that He commissions His servants to preach the Word, and, by voice and pen, expound the Scriptures; nevertheless, their labors will produce no eternal fruits, unless He condescends to bless the seed they sow and give it an increase. Thus, no matter how faithfully, simply, helpfully a sermon be preached or an article written, unless the Spirit *applies* it to the heart, the hearer or reader is no spiritual gainer. Then will you not humbly entreat God to open *your* heart to receive whatever is according to His holy Word in this chapter?

In what follows, we shall, as God enables, seek to direct attention to what we have referred to at the beginning of this discussion as the second of those two humanly insurmountable obstacles which lies in the way of a sinner's salvation, and that is the fitting of him for heaven, by the delivering of him from the power and presence of sin. Such a work is a divine one, and therefore is it *miraculous*. Regeneration is no mere outward reformation, no mere turning over a new leaf and endeavoring to live a better life. The new birth is very much more than going forward and taking the preacher's hand: it is a supernatural operation of God upon man's spirit, a transcendent wonder. All of God's works are wonderful. The world in which we live is filled with things which amaze us. Physical birth is a marvel, but, from several standpoints, the new birth is more remarkable. It is a marvel of divine grace, divine wisdom, divine power, and divine beauty. It is a miracle performed upon and within ourselves, of which we may be personally cognizant; it will prove an eternal marvel.

Because regeneration is the work of God, it is a *mysterious* thing. All God's works are shrouded in impenetrable mystery. Life, natural life in its origin, its nature, its processes, baffles the most careful investigator. Much more is this the case with spiritual life. The existence and Being of God transcends the finite grasp; how then can we expect to understand the process by which we become His children? Our Lord Himself declared that the new birth was a thing of mystery: "the wind bloweth where it listeth, and thou hearest the sound thereof, but *canst not tell* whence it cometh, and whither it goeth, *so* is every one that is *born* of the Spirit" (John 3:8). The wind is something about which the most learned scientist knows next to nothing. Its nature, the laws which govern it, its causation, all lie beyond the purview of human inquiry. So it is with the new birth: it is profoundly mysterious.

Regeneration is an intensely *solemn* thing. The new birth is the dividing line between heaven and hell. In God's sight there are but two classes of people on this earth: those who are dead in sins, and those who are walking in newness of life. In the physical realm there is no such thing as being *between* life and death. A man is either dead or alive. The vital spark may be very dim, but while it exists, life is present. Let that spark go out altogether, and, though you may dress the body in beautiful clothes, nevertheless, it is nothing more than a corpse. So it is in the spiritual realm. We are either saints or sinners, spiritually alive or spiritually dead, children of God or children of the devil. In view of this solemn fact, how momentous is the question, Have I been *born again?* If not, and you die in your present state, you will wish you had never been born at all.

2 The Necessity of Regeneration

A. *The need for regeneration lies in our natural degeneration.* In consequence of the fall of our first parents, all of us were born alienated from the divine life and holiness, despoiled of all those perfections wherewith man's nature was at first endowed. Ezekiel 16:4-5 gives a graphic picture of our terrible spiritual plight at our entrance into this world: cast out to the loathing of our persons, rolling ourselves in our own filth, impotent to help ourselves. That "likeness" of God (Gen. 1:26) which was at first stamped on man's soul had been effaced, aversion from God and an inordinate love of the creature having displaced it. The very fountain of our being is polluted, continually sending forth bitter springs, and though those streams take several courses and wander in various channels, yet are they all brackish. Therefore is the "sacrifice" of the wicked an abomination to the Lord (Prov. 15:8), and his very ploughing "sin" (Prov. 21:4).

There are but two states, and all men are included therein: the one a state of spiritual life, the other a state of spiritual death; the one a state of righteousness, the other a state of sin; the one saving, the other damning; the one a state of enmity, wherein men have their inclinations contrary to God; the other a state of friendship and fellowship, wherein men walk obediently unto God, and would not willingly have an inward motion opposed to His will. The one state is called darkness, the other light: "For ye were [in your unregenerate days, not only in the dark, but] darkness, but now are ye light in the Lord" (Eph. 5:8). There is no medium between these conditions; all are in one of them. Each man and woman now on earth is either an object of God's delight or of His abomination. The most benevolent and imposing works of the flesh cannot please Him, but the faintest sparks proceeding from that which grace hath kindled are acceptable in His sight.

By the fall man contracted an *unfitness* to that which is good. Shapen in iniquity and conceived in sin (Ps. 51:5), man is a "transgressor from the womb" (Isa. 48:8): "they go astray as soon as they be born, speaking lies" (Ps. 58:3), and "the imagination of man's heart is evil from his youth" (Gen. 8:21). He may be civilized, educated, refined, and even religious, but at heart he is "desperately wicked" (Jer. 17:9), and all that he does is vile in the sight of God, for nothing is done from love to Him, and with a view to His glory. "A good tree cannot bring forth evil fruit, neither can a corrupt tree bring forth good fruit" (Matt. 7:18). Until they are born again, all men are "unto every good work reprobate" (Titus 1:16).

By the fall man contracted an *unwillingness* to that which is good. All motions of the will in its fallen estate, through defect of a right principle from whence they flow and a right end to which they tend, are only evil and sinful. Leave man to himself, remove from him all the restraints which law and order impose, and he swiftly degenerates to a lower level than the beasts, as almost any missionary will testify. And is human nature any better in civilized lands? Not a whit. Wash off the artificial veneer and it will be found that "as in water face answereth to face, so the heart of man to man" (Prov. 27:19). The world over it remains solemnly true that "the carnal mind is enmity against God: for it is not subject to the law of God neither indeed can be" (Rom. 8:7). Christ will prefer the same charge in a coming day as when He was here on earth: "Men loved darkness rather than light" (John 3:19). Men *will not* come to Him that they might have life.

By the Fall man contracted an *inability* to do that which is good. He is not only unfitted and unwilling, but *unable* to do that which is good. Where is the man that can truthfully say he has measured up to his own ideals? All have to acknowledge there is a strange force within dragging them downward, inclining them to evil, which, notwithstanding their utmost endeavors against it, in some form or other, more or less, conquers them. Despite the kindly exhortations of friends, the faithful warnings of God's servants, the solemn examples of suffering and sorrow, disease and death on every side, and the vote that their own conscience gives, yet they yield. "They that are in the flesh [in their natural condition] *cannot* please God" (Rom. 8:8).

Thus it is evident that the need is imperative for a radical and revolutionary change to be wrought in fallen man before he can have any fellowship with the thrice holy God. Since the earth must be completely changed, because of the curse now resting on it, before it can ever again bring forth fruit as it did when man was in a state of innocency; so must man, since a general defilement from Adam has seized upon him, be renewed, before he can "bring forth fruit to God" (Rom. 7:4). He must be grafted into another stock, united to Christ, partake of the power of His resurrection; without this he may bring forth fruit, but not unto God.

How can anyone turn to God without a principle of spiritual motion? How can he live to God who has no spiritual life? How can he be fit for the kingdom of God who is of a brutish and diabolical nature?

B. *The need for regeneration lies in man's total depravity.* Every member of Adam's race is a fallen creature, and every part of his complex being has been corrupted by sin. Man's heart is deceitful above all things and desperately wicked (Jer. 17:9). His mind is blinded by Satan (II Cor. 4:4) and darkened by sin (Eph. 4:18), so that his thoughts are only evil continually (Gen. 6:5). His affections are prostituted, so that he loves what God hates and hates what God loves. His will is enslaved from good (Rom. 6:20) and opposed to God (Rom. 8:7). He is without righteousness (Rom. 3:10), under the curse of the law (Gal. 3:10) and is the captive of the devil. His condition is truly deplorable, and his case desperate. He cannot better himself, for he is "without strength" (Rom. 5:6). He cannot work out his salvation, for there dwelleth no good thing in him (Rom. 7:18). He needs, then, to be born of God, "for in Christ Jesus neither circumcision availeth anything, nor uncircumcision, but *a new creation*" (Gal. 6:15).

Man is a fallen creature. It is not that a few leaves have faded, but that the entire tree has become rotten, root and branch. There is in every one that which is radically wrong. The word *radical* comes from a Latin one which means "the root," so that when we say a man is radically wrong, we mean that there is in him, in the very foundation and fiber of his being, that which is intrinsically corrupt and essentially evil. Sins are merely the fruit, there must of necessity be a root from which they spring. It follows, then, as an inevitable consequence that man needs the aid of a Higher Power to effect a radical change in him. There is only One who can effect that change: God created man, and God alone can re-create him. Hence the imperative demand, "Ye *must* be born again" (John 3:7). Man is spiritually *dead* and naught but almighty power can make him alive.

"By one man sin entered into the world, and death by sin; and so death passed upon all men" (Rom. 5:12). In the day that Adam ate of the forbidden fruit, he died spiritually, and a person who is spiritually dead cannot beget a child who possesses spiritual life. Therefore, all by natural descent enter this world "alienated from the life of God" (Eph. 4:18), "dead in trespasses and sins" (Eph. 2:1). This is no mere figure of speech, but a solemn fact. Every child is born entirely destitute of a single spark of spiritual life, and therefore if ever it is to enter the kingdom of God, which is the realm of spiritual life (Rom. 14:17), it must be *born* into it.

The more clearly we are enabled to discern the imperative *need* of regeneration and the various reasons *why* it is absolutely essential in order for a fallen creature to be fitted for the presence of the thrice holy God, the less difficulty are we likely to encounter when we endeavor to arrive at an understanding of the *nature* of regeneration, *what* it is which takes place within a person when the Holy Spirit renews him. For this reason particularly, and also because such a cloud of error has been cast upon this vital truth, we feel that further study needs to be devoted to this particular aspect of our subject.

Jesus Christ came into this world to glorify God and to glorify Himself by redeeming a people unto Himself. But what glory can we conceive that God has, and what glory would accrue to Christ, if there be not a vital and fundamental difference between His people and the world? And what difference can there be between those two companies but in a *change of heart,* out of which are the issues of life (Prov. 4:23): a change of nature or disposition, as the fountain from which all other differences must proceed—sheep and goats differ in nature. The whole mediatorial work of Christ has this one end in view. His priestly office is to reconcile and bring His people unto God; His prophetic, to teach them the way; His kingly, to work in them those qualifications and bestow upon them that comeliness which is necessary to fit them for holy converse and communion with the thrice holy God. Thus does He "purify unto himself a peculiar people zealous of good works" (Titus 2:14).

"Know ye not that the unrighteous shall not inherit the kingdom of God? Be not deceived" (I Cor. 6:9). But multitudes *are* deceived, and deceived at this very point, and on this most momentous matter. God has warned men that "the heart is deceitful above all things, and desperately wicked" (Jer. 17:9), but few will believe that this is true of *them.* Instead, tens of thousands of professing Christians are filled with a vain and presumptuous confidence that all is well with them. They delude themselves with hopes of mercy while continuing to live in a course of self-will and self-pleasing. They fancy they are fitted for heaven, while every day that passes finds them the more prepared for hell. It is written of the Lord Jesus that "He shall save his people *from* their sins" (Matt. 1:21), not *in* their sins; save them not only from the penalty, but also from the power and pollution of sin.

To how many in Christendom do these solemn words apply, "For he flattereth himself in his own eyes, until his iniquity be found to be hateful" (Ps. 36:2). The principal device of Satan is to deceive people into imagining that they can successfully combine the world with God, allow the flesh while pretending to the Spirit, and thus "make the best of both worlds." But Christ has emphatically declared that "no man can serve two masters" (Matt. 6:24). Many mistake the real force of those searching words: the true emphasis is not upon "two," but upon "serve"—none can *serve* two masters. And God requires to be "served"—feared, submitted unto, obeyed; *His* will regulating the life in all its details (see I Samuel 12:24-25). "Thou shalt worship the Lord thy God, and him *only* shalt thou *serve*" (Matt. 4:10).

C. *The need for regeneration lies in man's unsuitedness to God.* When Nicodemus, a respectable and religious Pharisee, yea, a "master in Israel," came to Christ, He told him plainly that "except a man be born again" he could neither see nor enter the "kingdom of God" (John 3:3, 5)—either the gospel-state on earth or the glory-state in heaven. None can enter the spiritual realm unless he has a spiritual nature, which alone gives him an aptitude for and capacity to enjoy the things pertaining to it; and this, the natural man has not. So far from it, he cannot so much as "discern" them (I Cor. 2:14). He has no love for them, nor desire after them (John 3:19). Nor can he desire them, for his will is enslaved by the lusts of the flesh (Eph. 2:2-3). Therefore, before a man can enter the spiritual kingdom, his understanding must be supernaturally enlightened, his heart renewed, and his will emancipated.

There can be no point of contact between God and His Christ with a sinful man until he is regenerated. There can be no lawful union between two parties who have nothing vital in common. A superior and an inferior nature may be united together, but never contrary natures. Can fire and water be united, a beast and a man, a good angel and a vile devil? Can heaven and hell ever meet on friendly terms? In all friendship there must be a similarity of disposition; before there can be communion there must be some agreement or oneness. Beasts and men agree not in a life of reason, and therefore cannot converse together. God and men agree not in a life of holiness, and therefore can have no communion together (condensed from S. Charnock).

We are united to the "first Adam" by a likeness of nature; how then can we be united to the "last Adam" without a likeness to Him from a new nature or principle? We are united to the first Adam by a living soul, we must be united to the last Adam by a quickening Spirit. We have nothing to do with the heavenly Adam without bearing a heavenly image (I Cor. 15:48-49). If we are *His* members, we must have the same nature which was communicated to Him, the Head, by the Spirit of God, which is *holiness* (Luke 1:35). There must be one "spirit" in both: thus it is written, "he that is joined to the Lord is one spirit" (I Cor. 6:17). And again God tells us, "If any man have not the Spirit of Christ he is none of his" (Rom. 8:9). Nor can anything be vitally united to another without life. A living head and a dead body is inconceivable.

There can be no communion with God without a renewed soul. God is incapable on His part, with honor to His Law and holiness, to have fellowship with such a creature as fallen man. Man is incapable on his part, because of the aversion rooted in his fallen nature. Then how is it possible for God and man to be brought together without the latter experiencing a thorough change of nature? What communion can there be between Light and darkness, between the living God and a dead heart? "Can two walk together, except they be agreed?" (Amos 3:3). God loathes sin, man loves it; God loves holiness, man loathes it. How then could such contrary affections meet together in an amicable friendship? Sin has alienated us from the life of God (Eph. 4:18), and therefore from His fellowship; life, then, must be restored to us before we can be instated in communion with Him. Old things must pass away, and all things become new (II Cor. 5:17).

Gospel-duties cannot be performed without regeneration. The first requirement of Christ from His followers is that they shall *deny self.* But that is impossible to fallen human nature, for men are "lovers of their own selves" (II Tim. 3:2). Not until the soul is renewed will self be repudiated. Therefore is the new-covenant promise, "I will take the stony heart out of their flesh, and will give them an heart of flesh" (Ezek. 11:19). All gospel-duties require a pliableness and tenderness of heart. Pride was the condemnation of the devil (I Tim. 3:6), and our first parents fell through swelling designs to be like God (Gen. 3:5). Ever since then, man has been too aspiring and too well opinionated of himself to perform duties in an evangelical strain, with that nothingness in himself which the gospel requires. The chief design of the gospel is to beat down all glorying in ourselves, that we should glory only in the Lord (I Cor. 1:29-31); but this is not possible till grace renews the heart, melts it before God, and molds it to His requirements.

Without a new nature we cannot perform gospel-duties *constantly.* "They that are after the flesh do mind the things of the flesh" (Rom. 8:5). Such a mind cannot long be employed upon spiritual things. Prickings of conscience, terrors of hell, fears of death, may exert a temporary influence, but they do not last. Stony ground may bring forth blades, yet for lack of root, they quickly wither away (Matt. 13). A stone may be flung high into the air, but ultimately it falls back to the earth; so the natural man may for a time mount high in religious fervor, but sooner or later it shall be said of him, as it was of Israel, "Their *heart* was not right with him, neither were they *steadfast* in his covenant" (Ps. 78:37). Many seem to begin in the Spirit, but end in the flesh. Only where *God* has wrought in the soul, will the work last forever (Eccles. 3:14; Phil. 1:6).

As regeneration is indispensably necessary to a gospel-state, so it is to a state of heavenly glory. "It seems to be typified by the strength and freshness of the Israelites when they entered into Canaan. Not a decrepit and infirm person set foot in the promised land: none of those that came out of Egypt with an Egyptian nature, and desires for the garlic and onions thereof, suffering from their old bondage, but dropped their carcasses in the wilderness; only the two spies who had encouraged them against the seeming difficulties. None that retain only the old man, born in the house of bondage; but only a new regenerate creature, shall enter into the heavenly Canaan. Heaven is the inheritance of the sanctified, not of the filthy:

'that they may receive an inheritance among them which are sanctified through faith that is in me' (Acts 26:18). Upon Adam's expulsion from paradise, a flaming sword was set to stop his reentering into that place of happiness. As Adam, in his forlorn state, could not possess it, we also, by what we have received from Adam, cannot expect a greater privilege than our root. The priest under the law could not enter into the sanctuary till he was purified, nor the people into the congregation: neither can any man have access into the Holiest till he be sprinkled by the blood of Jesus: Heb. 10:22" (S. Charnock).

Heaven is a prepared place for a prepared people. Said Christ, "I go to prepare a place for you" (John 14:2). For whom? For those who have, in heart, "forsaken all" to follow Him (Matt. 19:27). For those who love God (I Cor. 2:9); and they who love God, love the things of God: they perceive the inestimable value and beauty of spiritual things. And they who really love spiritual things, deem no sacrifice too great to win them (Phil. 3:8). But in order to love spiritual things, the man himself must be made spiritual. The natural man may hear about them and have a correct idea of the doctrine of them, but he receives them not spiritually in the *love* of them (II Thess. 2:10), and finds not his joy and happiness in them. But the renewed soul longs after them, not by constraint, but because God has won his heart. His confession is, "Whom have I in heaven but thee? and there is none upon earth that I desire beside thee" (Ps. 73:25). God has become his chief good, His will is his only rule, His glory his chief end. In such an one, the very inclinations of the soul have been changed.

The man himself must be changed before he is prepared for heaven. Of the regenerate it is written, "giving thanks unto the Father, which hath *made us meet* to be partakers of the inheritance of the saints in light" (Col. 1:12). None are "made meet" while they are unholy, for it is an inheritance of the *saints;* none are fitted for it while they are under the power of darkness, for it is an inheritance *in light.* Christ Himself ascended not to heaven to take possession of His glory till after His resurrection from the dead, nor can we enter heaven unless we have been resurrected from sin. "He that hath wrought [polished] us *for* the selfsame thing [to be clothed with our heavenly house] is God," and the proof that He has done this is, the giving unto us "the earnest of the Spirit" (II Cor. 5:5); and where the Spirit of the Lord is "there is *liberty*" (II Cor. 3:17), liberty from the power of indwelling sin, as the verse which follows clearly shows.

"Blessed are the pure in heart: for they shall see God" (Matt. 5:8). To "see" God is to be introduced into the most intimate intercourse with Him. It is to have that "thick cloud" of our transgressions blotted out (Isa. 44:22), for it was our iniquities which separated between us and our God (Isa. 58:2). To "see" God, here has the force of *enjoy,* as in John 3:36. But for this enjoyment a "pure heart" is indispensable. Now the heart is purified by faith (Acts 15:9), for faith has to do with God. Thus, a "pure" heart is one that has been cleansed from sin and has a holy Object before it. A "pure" heart is one that has its affections set upon things above, being attracted by "the beauty of holiness." But how could he enjoy *God* who cannot now endure the imperfect holiness of His children, but rails against it as unnecessary "strictness" or puritanic fanaticism? God's face is only to be beheld in righteousness (Ps. 17:15).

"Follow peace with all and holiness, without which no man shall see the Lord" (Heb. 12:14). None can dwell with God and be eternally happy in His presence unless a radical change has been wrought in him, a change from sin to holiness. This change *must* be, like that introduced by the Fall, one which reaches to the very roots of our beings, affecting the entire man: removing the darkness of our minds, awakening and then pacifying the conscience, spiritualizing our affections, converting the will, reforming our whole life. And this great change must take place here on earth. The removal of the soul to heaven is no substitute for regeneration. It is not the *place* which conveys likeness to God. When the angels fell, they were in heaven, but the glory of God's dwelling place did not restore them. Satan entered heaven (Job 2:1), but he left it again unchanged. There must be a likeness to God wrought in the soul by the Spirit before it is fitted to enjoy heaven.

"Flesh and blood cannot inherit the kingdom of God" (I Cor. 15:50). If the body must be changed ere it can enter heaven, how much more so the soul, for "there shall in no wise enter into it anything that defileth" (Rev. 21:27). And *what is* the supreme glory of heaven? Is it freedom from toil and worry, sickness and sorrow, suffering and death? No; it is that heaven is the place where there is the full manifestation of Him who is "glorious in holiness"—that holiness which the wicked, while presumptuously hoping to go to heaven, despise and hate here on earth. The inhabitants of heaven are given a clear sight of the ineffable purity of God and are granted the most intimate communion with Him. But none are fitted for this unless their inner beings (as well as outer lives) have undergone a radical, revolutionizing, supernatural change.

Can it be thought that Christ will prepare mansions of glory for those who refuse to receive Him into their hearts and give Him the first place in their lives down here? No, indeed; rather will He laugh at their calamity and mock when their fear cometh (Prov. 1:26). The instrument of the heart must be tuned here on earth to fit it to produce the melody of praise in heaven. God has so linked together holiness and happiness (as He has sin and wretchedness) that they cannot be separated. Were it possible for an unregenerate soul to enter heaven, it would find there no sanctuary from the lashings of conscience and the tormenting fire of God's holiness. Many suppose that nothing but the *merits* of Christ are needed to qualify them for heaven. But this is a great mistake. None receive remission of sins through the blood of Christ who are not first "turned from the power of Satan unto God" (Acts 26:18). God subdues their iniquities whose sins He casts into the depths of the sea (Mic. 7:19). Pardoning sins and purifying the heart are as inseparable as the blood *and* water which flowed from the Saviour's side (John 19:34).

Our being renewed in the spirit of our mind, and our putting on of the new man "which after God is created in righteousness and true holiness" (Eph. 4:23-24) is as indispensable to a *meetness* for heaven, as having the righteousness of Christ imputed to us is for a *title* thereto. "A malefactor, by pardon, is in a *capacity* to come into the presence of a prince and serve him at his table, but he is not in the *fitness* till his noisome garments, full of vermin be taken off" (S. Charnock). It is both a fatal delusion and wicked presumption for one who is living to please self to imagine that *his* sins have been forgiven by God. It is the "washing of regeneration" which gives evidence of our being justified by grace (Titus 3:5-7). When Christ saves, He *indwells* (Gal. 2:20), and it is impossible for Him to reside in a heart which yet remains spiritually cold, hard, and lifeless. The supreme Pattern of holiness cannot be a Patron of licentiousness.

Justification and sanctification are inseparable: where one is absolved from the guilt of sin, he is also delivered from the dominion of sin, but neither the one nor the other can be until the soul is regenerated. Just as Christ's being made in the likeness of sin's flesh was indispensable for God to impute to Him His people's sins (Rom. 8:3), so it is equally necessary for us to be made new creatures in Christ (II Cor. 5:17) before we can be, legally, made the righteousness of God in Him (II Cor. 5:21). The need of our being made "partakers of the divine nature" (II Peter 1:4) is as real and as great as Christ's taking part in human nature, ere He could save us (Heb. 2:14-17). "Except God be born, He could not come into the kingdom of sin. Except a man be born again he cannot see the kingdom of righteousness. And divine power—the power of the Holy Spirit, the plenipotentiary and executant of all the will of Godhead—achieves the incarnation of God and the regeneration of man, that the Son of God may be made sin, and the sons of men made righteous" (H. Martin).

How could one possibly enter a world of ineffable holiness who has spent all of his time in sin, i.e., pleasing *self*? How could he possibly sing the song of the Lamb if his *heart* has never been tuned unto it? How could he endure to behold the awful majesty of God *face to face,* who never before so much as saw Him "through a glass darkly" by the eye of faith? As it is excruciating torture for eyes that have been long confined to dismal darkness, to suddenly gaze upon the bright beams of the midday sun, so will it be when the unregenerate behold Him who is Light. Instead of welcoming such a sight "*all* kindreds of the earth shall *wail* because of him" (Rev. 1:7); yea, so overwhelming will be their anguish, they will call to the mountains and rocks, "Fall on us, and hide us from the face of him that sitteth on the throne, and from the wrath of the Lamb" (Rev. 6:17). And, my reader, *that* will be *your* experience, unless God regenerate you!

3 The Nature of Regeneration

When the Lord Jesus said, "That which is born of the flesh is flesh" (John 3:6), He not only intimated that every man born into this world inherits a corrupt and fallen nature and therefore is unfit for the kingdom of God, but also that this corrupt nature can never be anything else but corrupt, so that no culture can fit it for the kingdom of God. Its tendencies may be restricted, its manifestations modified by education and circumstances, but its sinful tendencies and affections are still there. A corrupt tree cannot bring forth good fruit, prune and trim it as you may. For good fruit, you must have a good tree or graft from one. Therefore did our Lord go on to say, "And that which is born of the Spirit is spirit." This brings us to consider the nature of regeneration.

We have now arrived at the most difficult part of our subject. Necessarily so, for we are about to contemplate the workings of *God.* These are ever mysterious, and nothing whatever can really be known about them, save what He Himself has revealed thereon in His Word. In endeavoring to ponder what He *has* said on His work of regeneration two dangers need to be guarded against: first, *limiting* our thoughts to any isolated statement thereon or any single figure the Spirit has employed to describe it. Second, reasoning from what He has said by *carnalizing* the figures He has employed. When referring to spiritual things, God has used terms which were originally intended (by man) to express material objects, hence we need to be constantly on our guard against transferring to the former erroneous ideas carried over from the latter. From this we shall be preserved if we diligently compare *all* that has been said on each subject.

In treating of the nature of regeneration much damage has been wrought, especially in recent years, by men confining their attention to a single figure, namely, that of the "new birth," which is only one of many expressions used in the Scriptures to denote that mighty and miraculous work of God within His people which fits them for communion with Him. Thus, in Colossians 1:12-13, the same vital experience is spoken of as God's having "*made us meet* to be partakers of the inheritance of the saints in light: who hath delivered us from the power of darkness, and hath translated us into the kingdom of his dear Son." Regeneration is the commencement of a new experience, which is so real and revolutionizing that the one who is the subject of this divine begetting is spoken of as "a new creature: old things are passed away, behold, all things are become new" (II Cor. 5:17). A new spiritual life has been imparted to the soul by God, so that the one receiving it is vitally implanted into Christ.

The nature of regeneration can, perhaps, be best perceived by comparing and contrasting it with what took place at the Fall, for though the person who is renewed by the Spirit receives more than what Adam lost by his rebellion, yet, the one is, really, God's answer to the former. Now it is most important that we should clearly recognize that no faculty was lost by man when he fell. When he was created, God gave unto man a spirit, a soul, and a body. Thus, man was a tripartite being. When man fell, the divine threat "In the day that thou eatest thereof, thou shalt surely *die*" was duly executed, and man died spiritually. But that does not mean that either his spirit or soul, or any part thereof, ceased to be, for in Scripture "death" never signifies annihilation, but is a state of separation. The prodigal son was "dead" while he was in the far country (Luke 15:24), because he was separated from his father. "*Alienated from* the life of God" (Eph. 4:18) describes the fearful state of one who is unregenerate; so does "she that liveth in pleasure is dead while she liveth" (I Tim. 5:6): that is, dead spiritually, dead Godward, while alive in sin—the spirit, soul, and body, each being *active against* God.

That which took place at the Fall was not the destruction of either portion of man's threefold being, but the vitiating or corrupting of them. And that, by the introduction of a new principle within him, namely, *sin,* which is more of a quality than a substance. By the Fall man became possessed of a sinful "nature." But let it be stated very emphatically that a "nature" is *not* a concrete entity, but rather that which characterizes and impells an entity or creature. It is the nature of gravitation to attract, it is the nature of the wind to blow, it is the nature of fire to burn. A "nature" is not a tangible thing, but a *principle of operation,* a power impelling to action. Thus, when we say that fallen man possesses a "sinful nature," it must not be understood that something as substantial as his soul or spirit was *added* to his being, but instead, that a principle of evil *entered* into him, which polluted and defiled every part of his constitution, as frost entering fruit spoils it.

At the Fall, man lost none of the faculties with which the Creator had originally endowed him, but he lost the power to *use* his faculties *God-*

ward. All desire Godward, all love for his Maker, all real knowledge of Him, was lost. Sin possessed him: sin as a principle of evil, as a power of operation, as a defiling influence, took complete charge of his spirit and soul and body, so that he became the "servant" or slave "of sin" (John 8:34). As such, man is no more capable of producing that which is good, spiritual, and acceptable to God, than frost can burn or fire freeze: "they that are in the flesh [remain in their natural and fallen condition] *cannot* please God" (Rom. 8:8). They have no power to do so, for all their faculties, every part of their being, is completely under the dominion of sin. So completely is fallen man beneath the power of sin and spiritual death, that the things of the Spirit of God are "foolishness" unto him, "neither can he know them" (I Cor. 2:14).

Now that which takes place at regeneration is the *reversing* of what happened at the Fall. The one born again is, through Christ and by the Spirit's operation, *restored to* union and communion with God; the one who before was spiritually dead, is now spiritually alive (John 5:24). Just as spiritual death was brought about by the entrance into man's being of a principle of evil, so spiritual life is the introduction of a principle of holiness. God communicates a *new principle,* as real and as potent as sin. Divine grace is now imparted. A holy disposition is wrought in the soul. A new temper of spirit is bestowed upon the inner man. But no new faculties are created within him, rather are his original faculties enriched, ennobled, and empowered. Just as man did not become less than a threefold being when he fell, so he does not become more than a threefold being when he is renewed. Nor will he in heaven itself; his spirit and soul and body will simply be glorified, i.e., completely delivered from every taint of sin, and perfectly conformed to the image of God's Son.

At regeneration a "new nature" is imparted by God. But again we need to be closely on our guard lest we carnalize our conception of what is denoted by that expression. Much confusion has been caused through failure to recognize that it is a *person,* and not merely a "nature," which is born of the Spirit: "*ye* must be born again" (John 3:7), not merely something *in* you must be; "*he* which is born of God" (I John 3:9). The *same* person who was spiritually dead—his whole being, alienated from God—is now made spiritually alive: his whole being, reconciled to God. This must be so, or otherwise there would be no preservation of the *identity* of the individual. It is the person, and not simply a nature which is born of God: "Of his own will begat he *us*" (James 1:18). It is a new birth *of* the individual himself, and not of something *in* him. The nature is never changed, but the person is—relatively, but not absolutely.

The *person* of the regenerate man is essentially the same as the person of the unregenerate: each having spirit and soul and body. But just as in fallen man there is *also* a principle of evil which has corrupted every part of his threefold being, which "principle" is his "sinful nature" (so called because it expresses his evil disposition and character, as it is the "nature" of swine to be filthy), so when a person is born again another and new "principle" is introduced into his being, a new "nature" or disposition, a disposition which propels him Godward. Thus, in both cases "nature" is a quality rather than a substance. "That which is born of the Spirit is *spirit*" must not be conceived of as something substantial, distinct from the soul of the regenerate, like one portion of matter added to another; rather is it that which *spiritualizes* all his inward faculties, as the "flesh" had carnalized them.

Again, "that which is born of the Spirit is spirit" is to be carefully distinguished from that "spirit" which every man has in addition to his soul and body (see Num. 16:22; Eccles. 12:7; Zech. 12:1). That which is born of the Spirit is not something tangible, but that which is spiritual and holy, and that is a quality rather than a substance. In proof of this, compare the use of the word "spirit" in these passages: in James 4:5 the inclination and disposition to envy is called "the *spirit* that dwelleth in us lusteth to envy." In Luke 9:55 Christ said to His disciples, "Ye know not what manner of *spirit* ye are of," thereby signifying, ye are ignorant of what a fiery *disposition* is in your hearts. (See also Num. 5:14; Hos. 4:12; II Tim. 1:7.) That which is born of the Spirit is a principle of spiritual life, which renovates all the faculties of the soul.

Some help upon this mysterious part of our subject is to be obtained by noting that in such passages as John 3:6, etc., "spirit" is contrasted with "flesh." Now it should scarcely need saying that "the flesh" is not a concrete entity, being quite distinct from the body. When the term "flesh" is used in a moral sense the reference is always to the *corruption* of fallen man's nature. In Galatians 5:19-21 the "works of the flesh" are described, among them being "hatred" and "envyings," in connection with which the body (as distinguished from the mind) is *not* implicated—clear proof that the "flesh" and the "body" are not synonymous terms. In Galatians 5 the "flesh" is used to designate those evil tendencies and affections which result in the sins there mentioned. Thus, the "flesh" refers to the *degenerate state* of man's spirit and soul and body, as the "spirit" refers to the regenerate state of the spirit and soul—the regeneration of the body being yet future.

The privative (darkness is the privative of light) or negative side of regeneration is that divine grace gives a mortal wound to indwelling sin. Sin is not then eradicated nor totally slain in the believer, but it is divested of its *reigning* power over his faculties. The Christian is no longer the helpless slave of sin, for he resists it, fights against it, and to speak of a *helpless* victim "fighting," is a contradiction in terms. At the new birth sin receives its deathblow, though its dying struggles within us are yet powerful, and acutely felt. Proof of what we have said is found in the fact that while sin's solicitations were once agreeable to us, they are now hated. *This* aspect of regeneration is presented in Scripture under a variety of figures, such as the taking away of the heart of stone (Ezek. 36:26), the binding of the strong man (Matt. 12:29), etc. The absolute dominion of sin over us is destroyed by God (Rom. 6:14).

The positive side of regeneration is that divine grace effects a complete change in the state of the soul by infusing a principle of spiritual life, which renovates all its faculties. It is this which constitutes its subject a "new creature," *not* in respect of his essence, but of his views, his desires, his aspirations, his habits. Regeneration or the new birth is the divine communication of a powerful and revolutionizing principle into the soul and spirit, under the influence of which all their native faculties are exercised in a different manner from that in which they were formerly employed, and in *this* sense "old things are passed away; behold, all things are become new" (II Cor. 5:17). His thoughts are "new," the objects of his choice are "new," his aims and motives are "new," and thereby the whole of his external deportment is changed.

"By the grace of God I am what I am" (I Cor. 15:10). The reference here is to *subjective* grace. There is an objective grace, inherent in God, which is His love, favor, goodwill for His elect. There is also a subjective grace which terminates on them, whereby a change is wrought in them. This is by the infusion of a principle of spiritual life, which is the spring of the Christian's actions. This "principle" is called "a new heart" and a "new spirit" (Ezek. 36:26). It is a supernatural habit, residing in every faculty and power of the soul, as a principle of holy and spiritual operation. Some have spoken of this supernatural experience as a "change of heart." If by this expression be meant that there is a change wrought in the fallen nature itself, as though that which is natural is transformed into that which is spiritual, as though that which was born of the flesh *ceased to be* "flesh," and became that which is born of the Spirit, then the term is to be rejected. But if by this expression be meant an acknowledgment of the reality of the divine work which is wrought in those whom God regenerates, it is quite permissible.

When treating of regeneration under the figure of the new birth, some writers have introduced analogies from natural birth which Scripture by no means warrants, in fact disallows. Physical birth is the bringing forth into this world of a creature, a complete personality, which before conception had no existence whatever. But the one who is regenerated *had* a complete personality before he was born again. To this statement it may be objected, Not a *spiritual* personality! What is meant by this? Spirit and matter are opposites, and we only create confusion if we speak or think of that which is *spiritual* as being something concrete. Regeneration is not the creating of a person which hitherto had no existence, but the renewing and restoring of a person whom sin had unfitted for communion with God, and this by the communication of a nature or principle or life, which gives a new and different bias to all his old faculties. It is an altogether erroneous view to regard a Christian as made up of two distinct personalities.

As "justification" describes the change in the Christian's *objective* relationship to God, so "regeneration" denotes that intrinsic *subjective* change which is wrought in the inclinations and tendencies of his soul Godward. This saving work of God *within* His people is likened unto a "birth" because it is the gateway into a new world, the beginning of an entirely new experience, and also because as the natural birth is an issuing from a place of darkness and confinement (the womb) into a state of light and liberty, so is the experience of the soul when the Spirit quickens us. But the very fact that this revolutionizing experience is *also* likened unto a *resurrection* (I John 3:14) should deliver us from forming a one-sided conception of what is meant by the "new birth" and the "new creature," for resurrection is not the absolute creation of a new body, but the restoration and glorification of the old body. Regeneration is also called a divine "begetting" (I Peter 1:3), because the image or likeness of the Begetter is conveyed and stamped upon the soul. As the first Adam begat a son in his own image and likeness (Gen. 5:3), so the last Adam has an "image" (Rom. 8:29) to convey to His sons (Eph. 4:24; Col. 3:10).

It has often been said that in the Christian there are two distinct and diverse "natures," namely, the "flesh" and the "spirit" (Gal. 5:17). This is true; yet care must be taken to avoid regarding these two "natures" as anything more than two *principles* of action. Thus, in Romans 7:23 the two "natures" or "principles" in the Christian are spoken of as, "I see another *law* in my members, warring against the *law* of my mind." The flesh and the spirit in the believer must be conceived of as something very different from the "two natures" in the blessed person of our Redeemer, the God-man. Both the Deity and humanity *were* substantial entities in Him. Moreover, the "two natures" in the saint result in a necessary conflict (Gal. 5:17), whereas in Christ there was not only complete harmony, but "*one* Lord."

The faculties of the Christian's soul remain the same in their essence, substance, and natural powers as before he was "renewed," but these faculties *are* changed in their properties, qualities, and inclinations. It may help us to obtain a clearer conception of this if we illustrate by a reference to the waters at Marah (Exod. 15:25-26). Those "waters" were the same waters still, both before and after their cure. Of themselves, in their own nature, they were "bitter," so the people could not drink of them; but in the casting of a tree into them, they were made sweet and useful. So too with the waters at Jericho (II Kings 19:20-21), which were cured by the

4 The Effects of Regeneration

All men are by nature the children of wrath, and belong to the world, which is the kingdom of Satan (I John 5:19), and are under the power of darkness. In this state men are not the subjects of Christ's kingdom, and have no meetness for heaven. From this terrible state they are unable to deliver themselves, being "without strength" (Rom. 5:6). Out of this state God's elect are supernaturally "called" (I Peter 2:9), which call effectually delivers them from the power of Satan and translates them into the kingdom of God's dear Son (Col. 1:13). This divine "call," or work of grace, is variously denominated in Scripture: sometimes by "regeneration" (Titus 3:5), or the new birth, sometimes by illumination (II Cor. 4:6), by transformation (II Cor. 3:18), by spiritual resurrection (John 5:24). This inward and invincible call is attended with justification and adoption (Rom. 8:30; Eph. 1:5), and is carried on by sanctification in holiness. This leads us to consider the effects of regeneration.

"The wind bloweth where it listeth, and thou hearest the sound thereof, but canst not tell whence it cometh, and whither it goeth: so is every one that is born of the Spirit" (John 3:8). Though the wind be imperious in its action, man being unable to regulate it; though it be mysterious in its nature, man knowing nothing of the cause which controls it; yet its presence is unmistakable, its effects are plainly evidenced: so it is with *every one* that is born of the Spirit. His secret but powerful operations lie beyond the reach of our understanding. Why God has ordained that the Spirit should quicken this person and not that, we know not, but the transforming results of His working are plain and palpable. What these are, we shall now endeavor to describe.

A. *The illumination of the understanding.* As it was in the old creation, so it is in connection with the new. "In the beginning God created the heaven and the earth" (Gen. 1:1). That was the original creation. Then

29

came degeneration: "And the earth became without form and void [a desolate waste] and darkness was upon the face of the deep." Next came restoration: "And the Spirit of God moved upon the face of the waters, and God said, Let there be light: and there was light." So it is when God begins to restore fallen man: "For God who commanded the light to shine out of darkness, hath shined in our hearts, to give the light of the knowledge of the glory of God in the face of Jesus Christ" (II Cor. 4:6).

This divine illumination which the mind receives at the new birth is not by means of dreams or visions, nor does it consist in the revelation of things to the soul which have not been made known in the Scriptures. The only means or instrument which the Holy Spirit employs is the written Word: "The entrance of thy words giveth light; it giveth understanding unto the simple" (Ps. 119:130). Hitherto, God's Word may have been read attentively, and much of its teaching intellectually apprehended; but because there was a veil upon the heart (II Cor. 3:15) and so no spiritual discernment (I Cor. 2:14), the reader was not inwardly affected thereby. But now the Spirit removes that veil, opens the heart to receive the Word (Acts 16:14), and powerfully applies to the mind and conscience some portion of it. The result is that the one renewed is able to say, "One thing I know, that, whereas I was blind, now I see" (John 9:25). To particularize:

The sinner is now enlightened in the knowledge of his own terrible condition. He may, before this, have received much Scriptural instruction, subscribed to a sound creed, and believed intellectually in "the total depravity of man"; but now the solemn declarations of God's Word concerning the state of the fallen creature are brought home in piercing power to his own soul. No longer does he compare himself with his fellows, but measures himself by the rule of God. He now discovers that *he* is unclean, that his heart is "desperately wicked," and that he is altogether unfit for the presence of the thrice holy God. He is powerfully convicted of his own awful sins, feels that they are more in number than the hairs of his head, and that they are high provocations against heaven, which call for divine judgment on him. He now realizes that there is "*no* soundness" (Isa. 1:6) in him, and that all his best performances are only as "filthy rags" (Isa. 64:6), and that he is deserving of nought but the everlasting burnings.

By the spiritual light which God communicates in regeneration the soul now perceives the infinite demerits of sin, that its "wages" can be nothing less than eternal death, or the loss of divine favor and a dreadful suffering under the wrath of God. The equity of God's law and the fact that sin righteously calls for such terrible punishment is humbly acknowledged. Thus his mouth is "stopped" and he confesses himself to be guilty before God, and justly liable to His awful vengeance, both for the plague of his own heart and his numerous transgressions. He now realizes that his whole life has been lived in utter independence of God, having had no respect for His glory, no concern whether he pleased or displeased Him. He now perceives the exceeding sinfulness of sin, its awful malignity, as being in its nature contrary to the law of God. How to escape the due reward of his iniquity, he knows not. "What must I do to be saved?" is his agonizing cry. He is convinced of the absolute impossibility of contributing anything to his deliverance. He no longer has any confidence in the flesh; he has been brought to the end of himself.

By means of this illumination the renewed soul, under the guidance of the Spirit through the Word, now perceives how well suited is Christ to such a poor, worthless wretch as he feels himself to be. The prospect of obtaining deliverance from the wrath to come through the vicarious life and death of the Lord Jesus, keeps his soul from being overwhelmed with grief and from sinking into complete despondency because of the sight of his sins. As the Spirit presents to him the infinite merits of Christ's obedience and righteousness, His tender compassion for sinners, His power to save, desires for an interest in Christ now possess his heart, and he is resolved to look for salvation in no other. Under the benign influences of the Holy Spirit, the soul is drawn by some such words as, "Come unto me all ye that labor and are heavy laden, and I will give you rest," or "Him that cometh to me I will in no wise cast out," and he is led to apply to Him for pardon, cleansing, peace, righteousness, strength.

Other acts besides turning to Christ flow from this new principle received at regeneration, such as *repentance*, which is a godly sorrow for sin, an abhorring of it as sin, and an earnest desire to forsake and be completely delivered from its pollution. In the light of God, the renewed soul now perceives the utter vanity of the world, and the worthlessness of those paltry toys and perishing trifles which the godless strive so hard to acquire. He has been awakened from the dream-sleep of death, and things are now seen in their true nature. Time is precious and not to be frittered away. God in His awesome majesty is an object to be feared. His law is accepted as holy, just, and good. All of these perceptions and actions are included in that holiness without which no man shall see the Lord. In some these actions are more vigorous than in others, and consequently, are more perceptible to a man's self. But the fruits of them are visible to others in external acts.

B. *The elevation of the heart.* Rightly does the Lord claim the first place: "He that loveth father or mother more than me is not worthy of me" (Matt. 10:37). "My son, give me thine heart" (Prov. 23:26) expresses God's claim. They "first gave their own selves to the Lord" (II Cor. 8:5) declares the response of the regenerate. But it is not until they are born again that any are spiritually capacitated to do this, for by nature men are "lovers of their own selves" and "lovers of pleasure more than lovers of

God" (II Tim. 3:2, 4). When a sinner is renewed, his affections are taken off his idols and fixed on the Lord (I Thess. 1:9). Hence it is written "with the heart [the affections] man believeth unto righteousness" (Rom. 10:10). And hence, also, it is written, "If any man *love not* the Lord Jesus Christ let him be accursed" (I Cor. 16:22).

"And the Lord thy God will circumcise thine heart, and the heart of thy seed, to love the Lord thy God with all thy heart" (Deut. 30:6). The "circumcising" of the heart is the "renewing" of it, severing its love from all illicit objects. None can truly love God supremely till this miracle of grace has been wrought within him. Then it is that the affections are refined and directed to their proper objects, He who once was despised by the soul, is now beheld as the "altogether lovely" One. He who was hated (John 15:18), is now loved above all others. "Whom have I in heaven but thee? and there is none upon earth that I desire besides thee" (Ps. 73:25) is now their joyous confession.

The love of God has become the governing principle of their life (II Cor. 5:13). What before was drudgery is now a delight. The praise of man is no longer the motive which stimulates action; the approbation of the Saviour is the Christian's highest concern. Gratitude moves to a hearty compliance with His will. "How precious also are *thy* thoughts unto me, O God" (Ps. 139:17) is now his language. And again, "The desire of our soul is to thy name, and to the remembrance of thee. With my soul have I desired thee in the night; yea, with my spirit within me will I seek thee early" (Isa. 26:8-9). So too the heart is drawn out to all the members of His family, no matter what their nationality, social position, or church connections: "We know that we have passed from death unto life, because we love the brethren" (I John 3:14).

C. *The emancipation of the will.* By nature, the will of fallen man is free in only one direction: away from God. Sin has enslaved the will, therefore, do we need to be "made free" (John 8:36). The two states are contrasted in Romans 6: "free from righteousness" (v. 20), when dead in sin; "free from sin" (v. 18), now that we are alive unto God. At the new birth the will is liberated from the "bondage of corruption" (Rom. 8:21; cf. II Peter 2:19), and rendered conformable to the will of God (Ps. 119:97). In our degenerate state the will was naturally rebellious, and its practical language was, "Who is the Lord, that I should obey him?" (Exod. 5:2). But the Father promised the Son, "Thy people *shall be willing* in the day of thy power" (Ps. 110:3), and this is accomplished when God "worketh in us both to will and to do of his good pleasure" (Phil. 2:13; cf. Heb. 13:21).

"A new heart also will I give you, and a new spirit will I put within you: and I will take away the stony heart out of your flesh, and I will give you an heart of flesh. And I will put my Spirit within you, and cause you to walk in my statutes, and ye shall seek my judgments, and do them" (Ezek. 36:26-27). This is a new-covenant promise (Heb. 8:10), and is made good in each renewed soul. The will is so emancipated from the power of indwelling sin as to be enabled to answer to the divine commands according to the tenor of the new covenant. The regenerated freely consent to and gladly choose to walk in subjection to Christ, being anxious now to obey Him in all things. His authority is their only rule, His love the constraining power: "If a man love me, he *will* keep my words" (John 14:23).

D. *The rectification of the conduct.* A tree is known by its fruits. Faith is evidenced by works. The principle of holiness manifests itself in a godly walk. "If ye know that he is righteous, ye know that every one that doeth righteousness is born of him" (I John 2:29). The deepest longing of every child of God is to please his heavenly Father in all things, and though this longing is never fully realized in this life—"*Not* as though I had *already* attained, either were already perfect" (Phil. 3:12)—nevertheless he continues "reaching forth unto those things which are before."

"Ye have obeyed from the heart that form of doctrine *whereto ye* were delivered" (Rom. 6:17, mar.). The Greek word for "form" here signifies "mold." Observe how this figure also presupposes the *same* faculties after the new birth as before. Metal which is molded remains the same metal as it was previously, only the fashion or form of it is altered. That metal which before was a dish, is now turned into a cup, and thus a new name is given to it (cf. Rev. 3:12). By regeneration the faculties of the soul are made suitable to God and His precepts, just as the mold and the thing molded fit one another. As before the heart was at enmity against every commandment, it is now molded to them. Does God say, "Fear me," the renewed heart answers, "I *desire* to fear thy name" (Neh. 1:11). Does God say, "Remember the sabbath day to keep it holy," the heart answers, "The sabbath day is my *delight*" (Isa. 58:13). Does God say, "Love one another," the new creature finds an instinct begotten within it to *do* so, so that real Christians are said to be "taught of God *to love* one another" (I Thess. 4:9).

A change will take place in the deportment of the most moral unconverted man as soon as he is born from above. Not only will he be far less eager in his pursuit of the world, more scrupulous in the selection of his company, more cautious in avoiding the occasions to sin and the appearances of evil, but he realizes that the holy eye of God is ever upon him, marking not only his actions, but weighing his motives. He now bears the sacred name of Christ, and his deepest concern is to be kept from everything which would bring a reproach upon it. His aim is to let his light so shine before men that they may see his good works and glorify his Father which is in heaven. That which occasions him the deepest distress is not the sneers and taunts of the ungodly, but that he fails to measure up to the standard God has set before him, and that conformity to it after which he so much yearns. Though divine grace may preserve him from outward falls, yet he is painfully conscious of many sins within: the risings of unbelief, the swellings of pride, the oppositions of the "flesh" to the desires of the "spirit." These occasion him deep exercises of heart and lead to humble and sorrowful confessions unto God.

It is of great importance that the Christian should have clear and Scriptural views of what he is *both* as the subject of sin and of grace. Though the regenerate are delivered from the absolute dominion of sin (Rom. 6:14), yet the principle of sin, the "flesh," is not eradicated. This is clear from Romans 6:12, "Let not sin therefore reign in your mortal body, that ye should obey it in the lusts thereof": that exhortation would be meaningless if there were no indwelling sin seeking *to* reign, and no lusts demanding obedience. Yet this is far from saying that a Christian *must* go on in a course of sinning: "Whosoever is born of God doth not commit sin; for his seed remaineth in him: and he cannot sin, because he is born of God" (I John 3:9), the reference there being to the regular practice and habit of sinning. Nevertheless, prayerful heed needs to be constantly paid to this word, "Awake to righteousness, and sin not" (I Cor. 15:34).

The experiences of Paul, both as the subject of sin and of grace, are recorded in Romans 7. A careful reading of verses 14-24 reveals the fact that grace had neither removed nor purified the "flesh" in him. And as the Christian today compares his own inner conflicts, he finds that Romans 7 describes them most accurately and faithfully. He discovers that in his "flesh" is no good thing and he cries, "O wretched man that I am." Though he longs for fuller conformity to the image of Christ, though he hungers and thirsts after righteousness, though he is under the influence and reign of grace, and though he enjoys real fellowship with God, yet at seasons (some more acutely felt than others) he feels that though with the mind he serves the law of God, yet with the flesh the law of sin. Yea, every experience of reading the Word, prayer, meditation, proves to him that he is, in his fallen nature, "carnal, sold under sin," and that when he would do good, evil is present with him. This is a matter of great grief to him, and causes him to "groan" (Rom. 8:23) and yearn the more for release from this body of death.

But ought not the Christian to "grow in grace"? Yes, indeed. Yet let it be said emphatically that growing "in grace" most certainly does not mean an increasing satisfaction with myself. No, it is the very opposite. The more I walk in the light of God, the more plainly can I see the vileness of the "flesh" within me, and there will be an ever-deepening abhorence of what I am by nature. "For to will is present with me, but how to perform that which is good I find not" (Rom. 7:18) is not the confession of an unbeliever, nor even of a babe in Christ, but of the most enlightened saint. The only relief from this distressing discovery and the only peace for the renewed heart is to look away from self to Christ and His perfect work for us. Faith empties of all self-complacency and gives an exalted estimate of God in Christ.

A growth "in grace" is defined, in great part, by the words that immediately follow: " . . . and in the knowledge of our Lord and Saviour Jesus Christ" (II Peter 3:18). It is the growing realization of the perfect suitability of Christ to a poor sinner, the deepening conviction of His fitness to be the Saviour of such a vile wretch as the Spirit daily shows me I am. It is the apprehension of how much I need His precious blood to cleanse me, His righteousness to clothe me, His arm to support me, His advocacy to answer for me on high, His grace to deliver me from all my enemies both inward and outward. It is the Spirit revealing to me that there is *in Christ* everything that I need both for earth and heaven, time and eternity. Thus, growing in grace is an increasing living *outside* of myself, living *upon* Christ. It is a looking to Him for the supply of *every* need.

The more the heart is occupied with Christ, the more the mind is stayed on Him by trusting in Him (Isa. 26:3), the more will faith, hope, love, patience, meekness, and all spiritual graces, be strengthened and drawn forth into exercise and action to the glory of God. The *manifestation* of growth in grace and in the knowledge of Christ is another thing. The actual process of growing is not perceptible either in the natural or in the spiritual sphere; but the results of it are, mainly so to others. There are definite *seasons* of growth, and generally the Christian's spiritual graces are growing the most while the soul is in distress through manifold temptations, mourning on account of indwelling sin. It is when we are *enjoying* God and are in conscious communion with Him, feasting upon the perfections of Christ, that the fruits of the Spirit in us are *ripened.* The chief *evidences* of spiritual growth in the Christian are a deepening hatred of sin and loathing of self, a higher valuation of spiritual things, and yearning after them, a fuller recognition of our deep need and dependency on God to supply it.

Regeneration is substantially the same in all who are the subjects of it: there is a spiritual transformation, the conforming of the soul unto the image of God: "that which is born of the Spirit *is spirit*" (John 3:6). But although every regenerated person is a new creature, has received a principle of faith and holiness which acts on every faculty of his being, and is indwelt and led by the Holy Spirit, yet God does not communicate the same measure of grace (Rom. 12:3; II Cor. 10:13; Eph. 4:16) or the same number of talents to all alike. God's children differ from each other as children do at their natural birth, some of whom are more lively and vigorous than others. God, according to His sovereign pleasure, gives to

some fuller knowledge, to others stronger faith, to others warmer affections—natural temperament has much to do with the form and color which
the *manifestation* of the "spirit" takes through us. But there is no difference in their state: the same work has been performed in all, which radically differentiates them from worldlings.

"Do ye not know that the saints shall judge the world?" (I Cor. 6:2).
Does not this clearly denote, yea, require, that the "saints" shall exercise a
distinguishing holiness and live quite otherwise than the world? Could one
who now takes the Lord's name in vain be righteously appointed to sit in
judgment upon those who profane it? Could one who lives to please self be
a fit person to judge those who have loved pleasure more than God? Could
one who has despised and ridiculed "puritanic strictness of living" sit with
Christ as a judge on those who lived in rebellion against Him? Never;
instead of being the judges of others, all such will find themselves condemned and executed as malefactors in that day.

"The Lord will give grace and glory: no good thing will he withhold
from them that walk uprightly" (Ps. 84:11). "Grace and glory" are inseparably connected: they differ not in nature, but in degree. "Grace" is
glory begun; "glory" is grace elevated to its acme and perfection. In I John
3:2 we are told that the saints shall be "like him," and this, because they
will "see him as he is." The immediate vision of the Lord of glory will be a
transforming one, the bright reflections of God's purity and holiness cast
upon the glorified will make them perfectly holy and blessed. But this
resemblance to God, His saints do here, in measure, already bear: there are
some outlines, some lineaments of God's image stamped upon them, and
this too is through *beholding* Him. True, it is (comparatively speaking)
through a glass darkly, yet "beholding" we "*are* changed into the *same*
image from glory to glory [from one degree of it to another] as by the
Spirit of the Lord" (II Cor. 3:18).

Now let both writer and reader test and search himself in the presence
of God, by these questions: How stands my heart affected toward sin? Is
there a deep humiliation and godly sorrow after I have yielded thereto? Is
there a genuine detestation of it? Is my conscience tender, so that my
peace is disturbed by what the world calls "trifling faults" and "little
things"? Am I humbled when conscious of the risings of pride and self-
will? Do I loathe my inward corruption? What engages my mind in seasons
of recreation? Are my affections dead toward the world and alive toward
God? Do I find spiritual exercises pleasant and joyous or irksome and
burdensome? Can I truthfully say, "How sweet are thy words unto my
taste! yea, sweeter than honey to my mouth" (Ps. 119:103)? Is communion with God my highest joy? Is the glory of God dearer to me than
all that the world contains?

5 The Essence of Regeneration

Regeneration is that which alone fits a fallen creature to fulfill his one great and chief duty, namely, to glorify his Maker. This is to be the aim and end in view in all that we do: "Whether therefore ye eat, or drink, or whatsoever ye do, do all to the glory of God" (I Cor. 10:31). It is the motive actuating us and the purpose before us which gives value to each action: "When thine eye [figure of the soul looking outward] is single [having only one object in view—the glory of God], the whole body is full of light; but when thine eye is evil, the body is full of darkness" (Luke 11:34). If the intention be evil, as it certainly is when the glory of God is not before us, there is nothing but "darkness," *sin,* in the whole service.

Now fallen man has altogether departed from what ought to be his chief end, aim, or object, for instead of having before him the honor of God, *himself* is his chief concern; and instead of seeking to please God in all things, he lives only to please himself or his fellow creatures. Even when, through religious training, the claims of God have been brought to his notice and pressed upon his attention, at best he only parcels out one part of his time, strength, and substance to the One who gave him being and daily loadeth him with benefits, and another part for himself and the world. The natural man is utterly incapable of giving supreme respect unto God, until he becomes the recipient of a spiritual life. None will truly aim at the glory of God until they have an affection for Him, none will honor Him supremely whom they do not supremely love. And for this, the love of God must be shed abroad in the heart by the Holy Spirit (Rom. 5:5), and this only takes place at regeneration. Then it is, and not till then, that self is dethroned and God is enthroned; then it is that the renewed creature is enabled to comply with God's imperative call, "My son, give *me* thine heart" (Prov. 23:26).

The salient elements which comprise the *nature* of regeneration may, perhaps, be summed up in these three words: impartation, renovation, subjugation. God *communicates* something to the one who is born again, namely, a principle of faith and obedience, a holy nature, eternal life. This, though real, palpable, and potent, is nothing material or tangible, nothing added to our essence, substance, or person. Again, God *renews* every faculty of the soul and spirit of the one born again, not perfectly and finally, for we are "renewed day by day" (II Cor. 4:16), but so as to enable those faculties to be exercised upon spiritual objects. Again, God *subdues* the power of the sin indwelling the one born again. He does not eradicate it, but He dethrones it, so that it no longer has dominion over the heart. Instead of sin ruling the Christian, and that by his own willing subjection, it is resisted and hated.

Regeneration is *not* the improvement or purification of the "flesh," which is that principle of evil still with the believer. The appetites and tendencies of the "flesh" are precisely the same after the new birth as they were before, only they no longer *reign* over him. For a time it may seem that the "flesh" *is* dead, yet in reality it is not so. Often its very stillness (as an army, in ambush) is only awaiting its opportunity or a gathering up of its strength for a further attack. It is not long ere the renewed soul discovers that the "flesh" is yet very much alive, desiring to have its way. But grace will not suffer it to have its sway. On the one hand the Christian has to say, "For to will is present with me, but how to perform that which is good I find not" (Rom. 7:18). On the other hand, he is able to declare, "Christ liveth in me, and the life which I now live in the flesh I live by the faith of the Son of God, who loved me, and gave himself for me" (Gal. 2:20).

Some people find it very difficult to conceive of the *same* person bringing forth good works who before brought forth nothing but evil works, the more so when it be insisted upon that no new faculty is added to his being, that nothing substantial is either imparted or taken from his person. But if we rightly introduce the factor of *God's* mighty power into the equation, then the difficulty disappears. We may not be able to explain, in fact we are not, *how* God's power acts upon us, how He cleanses the unclean (Acts 10:15) and subdues the wolf so that it dwells with the lamb (Isa. 11:6), any more than we can thoroughly understand His working upon and within us without destroying our own personal agency; nevertheless, both Scripture and experience testify to each of these facts. It may help us a little at this point if we contemplate the workings of God's power in the natural realm.

In the natural realm every creature is not only entirely dependent upon its Maker for its continued existence, but also for the exercise of all its faculties, for "in him we live, and move [Greek "are moved"] and have our being" (Acts 17:28). Again, as the various parts of creation are linked together, and afford each other mutual support—as the heavens fertilize the earth, the earth supplies its inhabitants with food, its inhabitants propagate their kind, rear their offspring, and cooperate for the purpose of society—so also the whole system is supported, sustained, and governed by the directing providence of God. The influences of providence, the manner in which they operate on the creature, are profoundly mysterious; on the one hand, they are not destructive of our rational nature, reducing us to irresponsible automatons; on the other hand, they are all made completely subservient to the divine purpose.

Now, the operation of God's power in regeneration is to be regarded as of the same kind with its operation in providence, although it be exercised with a different design. God's energy is one, though it is distinguished by the objects on which, and the ends for which, it is exerted. It is the same power which creates as which upholds in existence: the same power which forms a stone and a sunbeam, the same power which gives vegetable life to a tree, animal life to a brute, and rational life to a man. In like manner, it is the same power which assists us in the natural exercise of our faculties, as it is which enables us to exercise those faculties in a spiritual manner. Hence "grace" as a principle of divine operation in the spiritual realm is the same power of God as "nature" is His process of operation in the natural world.

The grace of God in the application of redemption to the hearts of His people is indeed *mighty,* as is evident from the effects produced. It is a change of the whole man: of his views, motives, inclinations, and pursuits. Such a change no human means are able to accomplish. When the thoughtless are made to think and to think with a seriousness and intensity which they never formerly did; when the careless are, in a moment, affected with a deep sense of their most important interests; when lips which were accustomed to blaspheme, learn to pray; when the proud are brought to assume the lowly attitude and language of the penitent; when those who were devoted to the world give evidence that the object of their desires and aims is a heavenly inheritance; and when this revolution, so wonderful, has been effected by the simple Word of God, and by the very Word which the subjects of this radical change had often heard unmoved, it is proof positive that a mighty influence has been exerted, and that that influence is nothing less than *divine*—God's people have been made willing in the day of His *power* (Ps. 110:3).

Many figures are used in Scripture, various expressions are employed by the Spirit, to describe this saving work of God within His people. In II Peter 1:4 the regenerated are said to be "partakers of the divine nature," which does *not* mean of the very essence or being of God, for that can neither be divided nor communicated—in heaven itself there will still be an unmeasurable distance between the Creator and the creature, otherwise the finite would become infinite. No, to be "partakers of the divine nature" is to be made the recipients of inherent grace, to have the lineaments of the divine image stamped upon the soul: as the remainder of the verse shows, being "partakers of the divine nature" is the antithesis of "the corruption that is in the world through lust."

In II Corinthians 3:18 this transforming miracle of God's grace in His people is declared to be a "changing" into the image of Christ. The Greek word there for "change" is the one rendered "transfigured" in Matthew 17:2. At Christ's transfiguration no new features were added to the Saviour's face, but His whole countenance was irradiated by a new light; so in II Corinthians 4:6 regeneration is likened unto a "light" which God commands to shine in us—note the whole context of II Corinthians 3:18 is treating of the Spirit's work by the gospel. In Ephesians 2:10 this product of God's grace is spoken of as His "workmanship," and is said to be "created," to show that He, and not man, is the author of it. In Galatians 4:19 this same work of God in the soul is termed Christ's being "formed" in us—as the parents' seed is formed or molded in the mother's womb, the "likeness" of the parent being stamped upon it.

We cannot here attempt a full list of the numerous figures and expressions which the Holy Spirit has employed to set forth this saving work of God in the soul. In John 6:44 it is spoken of as a being "drawn" to Christ. In Acts 16:14 as the heart being "opened" by the Lord to receive His truth. In Acts 26:18 as an opening of our eyes, a turning us from darkness unto light, and from the power of Satan unto God. In II Corinthians 10:5 as the "casting down imaginations, and every high thing that exalteth itself against the knowledge of God, and bringing into captivity every thought to the obedience of Christ." In Ephesians 5:8 as being "light in the Lord." In II Thessalonians 2:13 it is designated the "sanctification of the Spirit." In Hebrews 8:10 as God's putting His laws into our mind and writing them on our hearts—*contrast* the figure in Jeremiah 17:1! Thus it should be most apparent that we lose much by limiting our attention to only one figure of it. All we have given, and still others not mentioned, need to be taken into consideration, if we are to obtain anything approaching an adequate conception of the *nature* of that miracle of grace which is wrought in the soul and spirit of the elect, enabling them henceforth to live unto God.

As man was changed in Adam from what he was by a state of creation, so man must be changed in Christ from what he is by a state of corruption. This change, which fits him for communion with God, is a divine work wrought in the inclinations of the soul. It is a being renewed in the spirit of our minds (Eph. 4:23). It is the infusion of a principle of holiness into all the faculties of our inner being. It is the spiritual renovation of our very persons, which will yet be consummated by the regeneration of our bodies. The whole soul is renewed according to the image of God in knowledge, holiness, and righteousness. A new light shines into the mind, a new power moves the will, a new object attracts the affections. The individual is the same, and yet not the same. How different the landscape when the sun is shining, than when the darkness of a moonless night is upon it—the same landscape, and yet not the same. How different the condition of him who is restored to fullness of health and vigor after having been brought very low by sickness; yet it is the same person.

The very fact that the Holy Spirit has employed the figures of "begetting" and "birth" to the saving work of God in the soul, intimates that the reference is only to the *initial* experience of divine grace: "He which hath *begun* a good work in you" (Phil. 1:6). As an infant has all the parts of a man, yet none of them as yet mature, so regeneration gives a perfection of parts, which yet have need to be developed. A new life has been received, but there needs to be a growth of it: "*grow* in grace" (II Peter 3:18). As God was the Giver of this life, He only can feed and strengthen it. Thus, Titus 3:5 speaks of "the renewing" and not the "renewal" of the Holy Spirit. But it is our responsibility and bounden duty to use the divinely appointed means of grace which promote spiritual growth: "*Desire* the sincere milk of the word that ye may grow thereby" (I Peter 2:2); as it is our obligation to constantly avoid everything which would hinder our spiritual prosperity: "Make not provision for the flesh to the lusts" (Rom. 13:14; cf. Matt. 5:29-30; II Cor. 7:1).

God's consummating of the initial work which we experience at the new birth, and which He renews throughout the course of our earthly lives, only takes place at the second coming of our Saviour, when we shall be perfectly and eternally conformed to His image, both inwardly and outwardly. First, regeneration; then our gradual sanctification; finally our glorification. But between the new birth and glorification, while we are left down here, the Christian has both the "flesh" and the "spirit," both a principle of sin and a principle of holiness, operating within him, the one opposing the other (see Gal. 5:16-17). Hence his *inward* experience is such as that which is described in Romans 7:7-25. As life is opposed to death, purity to impurity, spirituality to carnality, so is now felt and experienced within the soul a severe conflict between sin and grace. This conflict is perpetual, as the "flesh" and "spirit" strive for mastery. From hence proceeds the absolute necessity of the Christian being sober, and to "watch unto prayer."

Finally let it be pointed out that the principle of life and obedience (the new "nature") which is received at regeneration is not able to preserve the soul from sins, nevertheless, there is full provision for continual supplies of grace made for it and all its wants in the Lord Jesus Christ. There are treasures of relief in Him, whereunto the soul may at any time repair and find necessary succor against every incursion of sin. This new principle of holiness may say to the believer's soul, as did David unto Abiathar when he fled from Doeg: "Abide then with me, fear not; for him that seeketh my life, seeketh thy life; but with me thou shalt be in safeguard" (I Sam. 22:23). Sin is the enemy of the new nature as truly as it is of the Christian's soul, and his only safety lies in heeding the requests of that new nature, and calling upon Christ for enablement. This we are exhorted to in Hebrews 4:16. "Let us therefore come boldly unto the throne of grace, that we may obtain mercy, and find grace to help in time of need."

If ever there be a time of need with the soul, it is so when it is under the assaults of provoking sins, when the "flesh" is lusting against the "spirit." But at that very time there is suitable and seasonable help in Christ for succor and relief. The new nature begs, with sighs and groans, for the believer to *apply* to Christ. To neglect Him, with all His provision of grace, while He stands calling on us, *"Open* to me. . . . for my head is filled with dew and my locks with the drops of the night" (Song of Sol. 5:2), is to despise the sighing of the poor prisoner, the new nature, which sin is seeking to destroy, and cannot but be a high provocation against the Lord.

At the beginning, God entrusted Adam and Eve with a stock of grace in themselves, but they cast it away, and themselves into the utmost misery thereby. That His children might not perish a second time, God, instead of imparting to them *personally* the power to overcome sin and Satan, has laid up their portion in Another, a safe Treasurer; in Christ are their lives and comforts secured (Col. 3:3). And how must Christ regard us, if, instead of applying to Him for relief, we allow sin to distress our conscience, destroy our peace, and mar our communion? Such is not a sin of infirmity which cannot be avoided, but a grievous affront of Christ. The means of preservation from it is at hand. Christ is always accessible. He is ever ready to "succour them that are tempted" (Heb. 2:18). O to betake ourselves to Him more and more, day by day, for *everything.* Then shall each one find, "I *can* do all things through Christ which strengtheneth me" (Phil. 4:13).

PART TWO
Repentance

6 Introduction

One of the divinely predicted characteristics of the "perilous times" in which we are now living is that "evil men and seducers shall wax worse and worse, deceiving, and being deceived" (II Tim. 3:13). The deeper reference of these words is to *spiritual* seducers and deceivers. Men with captivating personalities, men who occupy prominent places in Christendom, men with an apparently deep reverence for Holy Writ, are beguiling souls with fatal error. Not only are evolutionists, higher critics, and modernists deluding multitudes of our young people with their sugar-coated lies, but some who pose as the champions of orthodoxy and boast of their ability to "rightly divide the Word of Truth," are poisoning the minds of many to their eternal destruction.

Such a charge as we have just made is indeed a serious one, and one which is not to be readily received without proof. But proof is easily furnished. The Word of God teaches plainly that in this dispensation, equally with preceding ones, God requires a sincere and deep repentance *before* He pardons any sinner. Repentance is absolutely necessary for salvation, just as necessary as is faith in the Lord Jesus Christ. "Except ye repent, ye shall all likewise perish" (Luke 13:3). "Then hath God also to the Gentiles granted repentance *unto life*" (Acts 11:18). "For godly sorrow worketh repentance *to salvation* not to be repented of" (II Cor. 7:10). It is impossible to frame language more explicit than that. Therefore, in view of these verses and others yet to be quoted we cannot but sorrowfully regard those who are now affirming that repentance is *not,* in this dispensation, essential unto salvation, as being deceivers of souls, blind leaders of the blind.

A careful comparison of the prominent place which is given to repentance in the New Testament with the very small place it has in present-day teaching, even in so-called "orthodox" pulpits, brings to light one of the

most significant and solemn "signs of the times." Some of the most prominent of those who are pleased to style themselves "teachers of *dispensational* truth" insist that repentance belongs to a past period, being altogether "Jewish," and deny in toto that, in this age, God demands repentance from the sinner before he can be saved, thus blankly repudiating Acts
17:30: "But *now* commandeth all men every where to repent." When it is
borne in mind that these men are most diligent students of Scripture, we
can but sorrowfully see in them the fulfillment of those words "ever
learning, and never able to come to the knowledge of the truth" (II Tim.
3:7).

Others, in their recoil from salvation by reformation, have failed to duly
preserve the balance of truth, and give proper place to such Scriptures as
"He that covereth his sins shall not prosper: but whoso confesseth and
forsaketh them shall have mercy" (Prov. 28:13), and "Let the wicked
forsake his way, and the unrighteous man his thoughts, and let him return
unto the Lord, and he will have mercy upon him" (Isa. 55:7). It is not
that there is anything meritorious in a sinner's compliance with this righteous demand of God, but that the claims of the Holy One must be pressed
on those who have transgressed against Him. Yet that is just the thing
which the haughty rebel desires to hear about least of all, and the sad thing
is that so many are now, wittingly or unwittingly, withholding that which
is unpalatable to men but which is honoring to God. How widespread this
withholding is may be quickly discovered by an examination of present-
day tracts purporting to explain *how* a sinner may be saved: in most of
them not a word is said about repentance! Alas, in the past, our own tracts
have failed sadly to sufficiently emphasize this point.

Even where it *is* held that repentance is necessary before a sinner can be
saved, only too often the most shallow and superficial views are entertained of what repentance really is. In many circles it is assumed that if a
person sheds tears or appears to be heartbroken on account of the evil
course he has followed, this is clear proof that a saving work of divine
grace has begun in that person's heart. But this by no means follows. The
prickings of an uneasy conscience are not the same as the conviction of sin
which is produced by the Holy Spirit. Esau wept, and wept bitterly, yet he
was not regenerated. Felix trembled under the preaching of Paul, but there
is no hint in Scripture that he has gone to heaven. Multitudes are deceived
on this very point, and there is very little in present-day ministry which is
calculated to undeceive them. Every one of us who values his soul and is
concerned about his eternal destiny, will do well to carefully examine his
repentance in the light of Scripture and ascertain whether it be of man or
from God, natural or supernatural.

The first occurrence of the word "repent" furnishes the key to its
meaning and scope. In Genesis 6:6 we read, "And it repented the Lord

that he had made man on the earth." The language is figurative, for He who is infinite in wisdom and immutable in counsel never changes His mind. This is plain from "God is *not* a man that he should lie, neither the son of man that he should repent" (Num. 23:19), and "The Strength of Israel will not lie *nor repent,* for he is not a man that he should repent" (I Sam. 15:29); and again, "with whom is *no* variableness, neither shadow of turning" (James 1:17). Thus, in the light of these definite statements we are compelled to conclude that in Genesis 6:6 (and similar passages) the Almighty condescends to accommodate Himself to our mode of speaking, and express Himself after a human manner—as He also does in Psalm 78:65; 87:6; Isaiah 59:16, etc.

Now by carefully noting the setting of this word in Genesis 6:6 and attentively observing what follows, we discover: first, that the *occasion* of repentance is *sin,* for in Genesis 6:5 we read that "God saw that the wickedness of man was great in the earth": thus repentance is a realization of the exceeding sinfulness of sin. Second, that the *nature* of repentance consists in a *change of mind:* a new decision is formed in view of the deplorable conditions existing—"it *repented* the Lord that he had made man." Third, that genuine repentance is *accompanied by* a real sorrow for sin, for that which necessitated the change of mind: "and it *grieved* him at his heart" (cf. II Cor. 7:10). Fourth, that the *fruit* or consequence of repentance appears in a determination to *undo* (forsake, and rectify as far as possible) that which is sorrowed over: "and the Lord said I will *destroy* man" (v. 7). All of these elements are found in a repentance which has been produced in the heart by the gracious and supernatural operation of the Holy Spirit.

7 The Necessity of Repentance

This is discovered by a contemplation of the law, for "by the law is the knowledge of sin" (Rom. 3:20). Where there is no enforcing and expounding of the holy law of God there can be no true, deep, saving knowledge of sin; as the apostle Paul so plainly affirms, "I had not *known* sin, but by the law" (Rom. 7:7). The exceeding sinfulness of sin (Rom. 7:13) is only exposed when the Spirit turns the light of God's law upon our conscience and heart. But this is preeminently an age of lawlessness, and that in every respect. And it cannot be otherwise: where the law of God is flouted, where thousands of preachers are declaring that the law has no place in this dispensation of grace, we cannot expect people to have much respect for human law. God has caused the people to reap that which they have sown: having sown the wind, they are now reaping the whirlwind. Bolshevism and anarchy are the inevitable rebound from having slighted and rejected the Ten Commandments!

Practical godliness consists in a conformity of heart and life to the *law* of God, and in a sincere compliance with the *gospel* of Christ. But it is only as we rightly understand both the law and the gospel that we can discern wherein a conformity to the one and a compliance with the other really consists. Now the requirements of the law are summed up in that word, "Thou shalt love the Lord thy God with all thine heart, and with all thy soul, and with all thy might" (Deut. 6:5; cf. Matt. 22:37). Observe carefully the three things here specified: first, the duty required, namely, love to God. Second, the ground or reason for this, namely, because He is the Lord our God. Third, the measure or extent of this duty, namely, to love Him with all the heart. Nothing other than this, nothing less than this, will ever meet the righteous claims of God upon us.

Now that which is implied in and required unto a real love to God is, first, a true *knowledge of Him*. If our apprehensions of God are wrong, if they are not formed by Scripture, then it is obvious we have but a false image of Him, framed by our own fancy. By a true knowledge of God (John 17:3; I John 5:20) we mean far more than a correct theoretical notion of His perfections: there must be a heartfelt realization of His personal loveliness, His ineffable glory. And where *that* truly exists, there will be a *delighting* of ourselves in Him (Ps. 37:4) and a desire and a determination to *please* Him. And self-love naturally causes us to magnify self and seek to promote our own interests, so a true love to God causes us to put Him first and seek His interests.

In repentance *sin* is the thing to be repented of, and sin is a transgression of the law (I John 3:4). And the first and chief thing required by the law is *supreme love to God.* Therefore, the lack of supreme love to God, the heart's disaffection for His character and rebellion against Him (Rom. 8:7) is our great wickedness, of which we have to repent. But it will never be in our hearts to repent unless we truly see our blame. And we can never truly see our blame until we perceive that which chiefly renders us *to* blame. It is the excellency of God, the infinite perfections of His glorious being, which renders Him worthy of and entitled to our supreme love and fullest obedience; and this it is which chiefly renders us to blame, for *not* having loved and served Him. Not to love so lovable an Object as the God of love is the crime of crimes.

What is *sin?* Sin is saying, I renounce the God who made me; I disallow His right to govern me. I care not what He says to me, what commandments He has given, nor how He expostulates: I prefer self-indulgence to His approval. I am indifferent unto all He has done to and for me; His blessings and gifts move me not: I am going to be lord of myself. Sin is rebellion against the majesty of heaven. It is to treat the Almighty with contempt. Oh, how vastly different a thing is *sin* from what the world supposes! How insensible are the unregenerate to the glory of God and that which is due unto Him from us!

The natural man supposes that the great evil of sin consists in its being so injurious *to us.* For a creature which is absolutely dependent to assume an attitude of haughty independence is the sin of sins. To despise One who is infinitely glorious and infinitely worthy of honor, love, and obedience, is an awful abomination. To be more concerned about pleasing fellow rebels than to seek the favor of God is turpitude of the blackest dye. O reader, if you have never seen the *great evil* of sin, then are you a stranger to God and blind to His surpassing loveliness; you are under the *blinding* power of sin.

Weigh well what is now being presented if you value your soul, dear friend. The "*deceitfulness* of sin" (Heb. 3:13) may hitherto have closed your eyes to the terrible condition you are in. If so, are you now willing to be undeceived? Are you willing to really see *yourself?* Then make no mistake upon this point: never was any sinner pardoned while he was impenitent; and never was a soul truly penitent while insensible of the great evil of sin; and never did a sinner perceive the great evil of sin till he became acquainted with the infinitely great and glorious God against whom he has sinned. You may indeed have been sorry for sin on *other* accounts—as exposing you to shame before men, as having injured your reputation, or because it has brought down God's chastening hand upon your body or temporal affairs. But if you have never seen the great evil of sin as it is against that God who is infinitely glorious in Himself, then your repentance was not genuine, and *God* has not pardoned you.

"Against thee, thee only, have I sinned, and done this evil in thy sight" (Ps. 51:4). A sense of the great evil of sin is essential to true repentance. We cannot be suitably affected toward things unless we see them as they are. No matter how lovely a thing or person may be, if their excellency be not perceived the heart is untouched. Even the infinite glory of God will not excite our esteem and love, if we have no sense of it. So, on the other hand, let sin be never so evil, yet if this be not *realized* we are not suitably affected toward it. Though it deserves to be hated with perfect hatred, and though there be every reason why we should be horrified on account of it and abase ourselves before God, mourning it in bitterness of heart, fearing it, watching against it as the greatest of all evils, yet we shall never do so until we see sin in its real hideousness. Thus a deep sense of the infinite evil of sin is plainly essential to repentance, yea, it is from this that repentance immediately springs.

The evil of sin arises from our obligations to do otherwise, namely, our being under obligation to love and serve Him who is infinitely glorious. But unless I clearly see this, there will not be, there cannot be any deep repentance. The language of every sinner's heart is, I care not *what* God requires, I am going to have *my own* way. I care not what be God's claims upon me, I refuse to submit unto His authority. I care not what He has threatened to do unto those that defy Him, I will not be intimidated. His eyes may be upon me, but I am not going to be restrained thereby; I care not what *He* loves and what He hates, I shall please myself. But when the Holy Spirit enlightens and convicts a soul, his language is—"Against thee, thee only, have I sinned, and done this evil in thy sight."

Thus, true repentance issues from a realization in the heart, wrought therein by the Holy Spirit, of the sinfulness of sin, of the awfulness of ignoring the claims of God and defying His authority. It is therefore a holy horror and hatred of sin, a deep sorrow for it, an acknowledgment of it before God, and a complete heart-forsaking of it. Not until this is done will God pardon us. Whoever will take the trouble to search through the Scriptures on this point, will find that it is plainly and uniformly taught by Moses and the prophets, by Christ and His apostles. Begin with what God demanded on the Day of Atonement: "whatsoever soul it be that shall not be *afflicted* in that same day," so far from the sacrifice removing *his* sins, "he shall be cut off from among his people" (Lev. 23:29).

Weigh well the teaching of these verses: "If they shall bethink themselves in the land whither they were carried captives, and *repent,* and make supplication unto thee in the land of them that carried them captives, saying, We have sinned, and have done perversely, we have committed wickedness; and *return* unto thee with *all* their heart, and with all their soul, in the land of their enemies, which led them away captive, and *pray* unto thee. . . , *then* hear thou their prayer and their supplication . . . and *forgive* thy people that have sinned against thee" (I Kings 8:47-50). No change of dispensation has wrought any change in the character of the thrice holy God. His claims are ever the same.

For the teachings of the prophets *see* Psalm 32:3-5; Proverbs 28:13; Jeremiah 4:4, Ezekiel 18:30-32, Hosea 5:15, Joel 2:12-13. John the Baptist, the forerunner of Christ, preached saying, "Repent ye, for the kingdom of heaven is at hand" (Matt. 3:2). This was as though he said, "Such is the nature of the Messiah's kingdom, so holy is it, that no impenitent sinner, while such, can be a member of it and share its blessings. The promised One is on the eve of making His appearance: therefore repent ye, and thus be prepared to receive Him." Thus did John preach, and many did he turn unto the Lord their God (Luke 1:16-17).

The Lord Jesus taught and constantly pressed the *same* truth. His call was, "Repent ye, and believe the gospel" (Mark 1:15): the gospel cannot be savingly believed until there is genuine repentance—as the ground must be ploughed before it is capable of receiving the seed, so the heart must be melted ere it will welcome the Lord and Saviour Jesus Christ. Therefore did He declare, "Blessed are they that *mourn,* for they shall be comforted" (Matt. 5:4), and announce that He had been sent "to heal the *brokenhearted*" (Luke 4:18). He came here to "call sinners to repentance" (Luke 5:32), and insisted that "except ye repent, ye shall all likewise perish" (Luke 13:3, 5). He illustrated this truth at length in the parable of the prodigal son, who "came to himself," repented, *left* the "far country," returned to the Father, and so obtained His forgiveness (Luke 15:17-20).

When risen from the dead, Christ commissioned His servants "that repentance *and* remission of sins should be preached in His name among *all* nations" (Luke 24:47), and Acts 5:31 tells us that He has been exalted on high to communicate these blessings in the *same order,* namely, "to give repentance to [the *spiritual*] Israel *and* forgiveness of sins." Accordingly we find the apostles, who were filled with the Holy Spirit, thus carrying out His command. On the day of Pentecost when many were "pricked in their hearts" and asked, "What shall we do?" Peter did not say, Do nothing, but rest upon the finished work of Christ. Instead, he said, "*Repent,* and be baptized every one of you in the name of Jesus Christ, for the remission of sins" (Acts 2:38). Again, in Acts 3:19 we find him saying, "Repent ye therefore and be converted *that* your sins *may* be blotted out"!

When Paul was converted and sent to preach the gospel to the Gentiles, it was to "open their eyes and to *turn them from* darkness to light and from the power of Satan unto God, *that* they might receive forgiveness of sins" (Acts 26:18); hence we find he went everywhere and preached to men that "they should repent and turn to God and do works meet for repentance" (Acts 26:20), "testifying to both Jews *and also* to the Greeks, repentance toward God and faith toward our Lord Jesus Christ" (Acts 20:21). As to those who shut their eyes, stopped their ears, hardened their hearts, and were given up to destruction in the days of the prophets (Isa. 6:10), of Christ (Matt. 13:15), and of the apostles (Acts 28:27), their sentence ran thus: " . . . lest they should see with their eyes, hear with their ears, understand with their hearts, and be converted, and I should heal them," which, compared with Mark 4:12, signifies, "and their sins should be forgiven them."

Against these clear and consistent testimonies of Holy Writ, certain men have insisted that the divine call to repentance was never made to any except those who were in covenant relationship with God. But as we have shown, Acts 17:30 and 26:20 clearly expose this error. Some have pointed out that the word "repent" is not once found in all John's Gospel, and in view of 20:31 have *reasoned* that it is not necessary unto salvation. But John's Gospel is plainly addressed unto those who are saved (see 1:16). It is that Gospel which sets forth the Son in relation to the sons of God. John 20:31 obviously means that this Gospel is written to strengthen the faith of believers; as I John 5:13 (addressed to those who already knew they were saved: see 2:3, etc.) signifies the purpose of that Epistle was to *deepen* assurance. Others have drawn a false inference from the very infrequent mention of repentance in the Epistles, but they also are addressed to the saints; yet II Corinthians 7:10; II Timothy 2:25, II Peter 3:9 manifestly confirm the fact that repentance is required throughout this dispensation.

"There is no *new* thing under the sun" (Eccles. 1:9), nor is the present-day denial of the necessity of repentance for salvation any twentieth-century novelty. In proof of this statement we could fill page after page with quotations from Antinominans and others who lived long before "dispensational truth" was first heard of. No, it is an old device of Satan's, yet under a new dress. But woe be unto those who accept his lie. God must cease to exist before He will lower His claims and cease demanding repentance from all who have rebelled against Him. Make no mistake upon this point, dear reader: it is turn or burn—turn from your course of self-will and self-pleasing; turn in brokenheartedness to God, seeking His mercy in Christ; turn with full purpose to please and serve Him, or be tormented day and night forever and ever in the lake of fire.

8 The Nature of Repentance

"Except ye repent, ye shall all likewise perish" (Luke 13:3). In view of these solemn words it is tremendously important that each of us should seek and obtain from God the repentance which He requires, not resting content with anything short of this. Hence, there needs to be the most diligent and prayerful examination as to the character of our repentance. Multitudes are deceived thereon. Many are perplexed by the conflicting teaching of men on this subject; but instead of that discouraging, it should stir up to a more earnest searching of the Scriptures. Before turning to the positive side of this branch of our theme, let us first point out some of the features of a nonsaving repentance.

Trembling beneath the preaching of God's Word is not repentance. True, there are thousands of people who have listened unmoved to the most awe-inspiring sermons, and even descriptions of the torments of the damned have struck no terror to their hearts. Yet, on the other hand, many who *were* deeply stirred, filled with alarm, and moved to tears, are now in hell. I have seen the faces of strong men pale under a searching message, yet next day all its effects had left them. Felix "trembled" (Acts 24:25) under the preaching of Paul!

Being "almost persuaded" is not repentance. Agrippa (Acts 26:28) is a case in point. A person may give full assent to the messages of God's servant, admire the gospel, yea, receive the Word with joy, and after all, be only a stony-ground hearer (Matt. 13:20-21). Not only so, he may be conscious of his evildoing and acknowledge the same. Pharaoh owned, "I have sinned against the Lord your God" (Exod. 10:16). A man may realize that he *ought* to yield himself to the claims of God and become a Christian, yet never be more than "*almost* persuaded."

Humbling ourselves beneath the mighty hand of God is not repentance. People may be deeply moved, weep, go home and determine to reform their lives, and yet return to their sins. A solemn example of this is found in Ahab. That wicked king of Israel coveted Naboth's vineyard, plotted to secure it, and gained his end by causing him to be murdered. Then the servant of God met him and said, "Hast thou killed and also taken possession?" And we are told that "he rent his clothes, and put sackcloth upon his flesh, and fasted . . . and went softly" (I Kings 21:27-29). Yet in the very next chapter we find him again rebelling against God, and that he was cut off by divine judgment. Ah, my reader, you may have humbled yourself before God for a time, and yet remain the slave of your lusts. You may be afraid of hell, and yet not of sinning. If hell were extinguished, so would be the repentance of many church members. O mistake not fear of the wrath to come for a holy hatred and horror of sin.

Confessing sins is not repentance. Thousands have gone forward to the "altar" or "mourners' bench" and have told God what vile creatures they were, enumerating a long list of transgressions, but without any deep realization of the unspeakable awfulness of their sins, or a spark of holy hatred of them. The sequel has shown this, for they now ignore God's commandments as much as they did before. O my reader, if you do not, in the strength of God, *resist* sin, if you do not *turn from it,* then your fancied repentance is only whitewash—paint which decorates, but not the grace which transforms into gold.

You may even do works meet for repentance, and yet remain impenitent. A sinner may be convinced of the evil of his ways, turn from them, and go so far as to make restitution for the harm which he has wrought, and yet perish notwithstanding. A clear proof of this is furnished in the New Testament. Judas confessed his sins to the priests, and returned their money (Matt. 27:3-5), and then he went out from the presence of those evil men. Was he saved? No, he went and hanged himself! O how this ought to make each of us tremble and search our hearts.

The Greek *metanoeo,* which occurs most frequently as the word rendered "repent," signifies a change of mind; Matthew 21:29 both illustrates and confirms that definition. Yet let it be said very emphatically that saving repentance means far more than a mere change of opinions: it is a *changed mind,* which leads to action. Now this changed mind is not brought about by any intellectual process, but is the result of the understanding being wrought upon by the conscience, and that as the conscience has been supernaturally ploughed up by the Holy Spirit. In consequence of this there is a judging or condemning of self, a taking sides with God against myself.

Fallen man is not now on trial, but is a criminal already under sentence (John 3:18). "There is none righteous, no, not one: There is none that understandeth, there is none that seeketh after God. They are all gone out of the way, they are together become unprofitable; there is none that doeth good, no, not one" (Rom. 3:10-12). *That* is God's indictment against each of us. No pleading will avail, no excuses will be accepted. The present issue between God and the sinner is, Will man bow to, or endorse with his heart, God's righteous verdict?

It is just here that the gospel meets us. It comes to us as those who are already *lost,* as those who are "ungodly," "without strength," at "enmity with God." When the gospel first comes to the sinner it finds him in a state of apostacy from God, both as sovereign Ruler and as our supreme Good, neither obeying and glorifying Him, nor enjoying and finding satisfaction in Him. Hence the demand for "repentance toward God" *before* "faith toward our Lord Jesus Christ" (Acts 20:21). True repentance toward God *removes* this disaffection of our minds and hearts toward Him, under both these characters. In saving repentance the whole soul turns to Him and says: I have been a disloyal and rebellious creature: I have scorned Thy high authority and most rightful law. I will live no longer thus. I now desire and determine with all my might to serve and obey Thee as my only Lord. I subject myself unto Thee, to submit to Thy will.

Nor is the above all that a truly penitent soul says to God. He goes on: Hitherto I have been a miserable and forlorn creature, destitute of anything which could satisfy or make me truly happy. My heart has been set upon a vain world, which could not meet my real needs: it has flattered and mocked me often, but never contented me; it has "pierced me through with many sorrows." I forsook the Fountain of living waters, and turned to broken cisterns which held none. I own and bewail my folly; I unsparingly condemn myself for my madness. I now betake myself to Thee as my present and everlasting Portion.

The gospel proclaims the amazing *grace* of God, which is the guilty and condemned sinner's *only* hope. Yet that grace will never be welcomed until the sinner really bows beneath God's sentence against him. This is why both repentance *and* faith are demanded of us. The two must never be separated. When our Lord was speaking to the chief priests and elders about their rejection of John's message, the charge He preferred against them was: Ye "repented not afterward, *that ye might believe* in him" (Matt. 21:32). Repentance is the heart's acknowledgment of the justice of God's sentence of condemnation; faith is the heart's glad acceptance of the grace and mercy which are extended to us through Christ. Repentance is not simply the turning over of a new leaf and a vowing that I will mend my ways: rather is it a setting to my seal that God is true when He declares I am "*without* strength": that in myself, my case is hopeless, that I am no more capable of "doing better" than I am of creating a world. Not until this is believed on the authority of God's Word shall I really turn to Christ and welcome Him—not as a Helper, but as Saviour!

Repentance is more than a conviction of sin or terror of the wrath to come. This is clear from Acts 2:37-38. Under Peter's searching message, the Jews were made to realize their awful guilt before God: they were made conscious of the fearful fact that they had murdered the Prince of life, and so were in terrible fear of being cast into hell. Nevertheless, though already "pricked in their hearts," when they cried out, "What shall we do?" Peter said, "Repent." To a superficial mind, such a demand might appear needless: yet was it seasonable counsel. Their being "pricked in their heart" was *legal terror,* whereas saving "repentance" is an *evangelical* judging of self, mourning over sin out of a sense of God's grace and goodness.

A prayerful and careful pondering of Acts 2:37-38 should correct more than one error which is now current in various circles. When the hearers of Peter were affrighted by their awful crime and fearful of eternal wrath, pricked in the heart—as though a sword had been run through their vitals—they cried out in anguish, "What shall we do?" The apostle did not say, "Be passive, there is nothing you can do," thus encouraging the fatal inertia of hyper-Calvinists. Nor did he say, "Believe your sins *are* blotted out," which is the counsel of many "physicians of no value" in our day. No, his reply was far otherwise, in substance amounting to this: "Take all the blame which belongs to you. Own the whole truth unto God. Do not gloss over, but confess your awful wickedness; let your uncircumcised hearts be truly humbled before Him. And then look by faith to the free grace of God through the blood of Christ for pardon, and in token that all your dependence is on His mediation and merits, be baptized in His name, and that shall be to you an *external sign* of the remission of your sins."

"It is manifest from the nature of the case, that he who hath his eyes opened to see the glory of the divine nature, the beauty of the divine law, the infinite evil of sin, the need of an infinite atonement, and so to see his need of Christ: and at the same time, views God as the supreme, all-sufficient Good, ready to receive every sinner that returns to Him through Christ; it is manifest, I say, that everyone who is thus taught of God, will repent and return to God as his sovereign Lord and supreme Good, and return through Jesus Christ, who is the way to the Father, and the only way, in the view of one thus divinely enlightened. For in the clearer light the glory of the divine nature and law is seen, in exact proportion will be the sense of the infinite evil of sin, and the need of Christ's infinite atonement and perfect righteousness. And so 'repentance toward God and faith toward our Lord Jesus Christ' will be naturally and inseparably connected. Yea, they will be necessarily implied in each other.

"He who repents in the view of the glory of God, the glory of the law, and of the atonement, will in his repentance look only to free grace through Jesus Christ for mercy, and he who looks only to free grace through Jesus Christ for mercy, in a view of the glory of God, law, atonement, will in doing so take the whole blame of his disaffection to the divine character, as exhibited in the law, and on the cross of Christ, to himself, *judging and condemning himself,* and in the very act of faith, repent and be converted. When, therefore, it is said, 'Believe on the Lord Jesus Christ, and thou shalt be saved' (Acts 16:31), *the same* (inclusive) *thing is meant* as when it is said, 'Repent ye therefore and be converted that your sins may be blotted out' (Acts 3:19). For the apostolic faith implies repentance in its own nature, and their repentance implies faith in its nature. Sometimes they only mention faith, and sometimes only repentance, and sometimes both together; but the *same thing* is *always* intended. For in the view of the apostles, repentance and faith were mutually implied in each other" (Jos. Bellamy, 1750).

Giving a more full and formal definition of repentance, we would say: Repentance is a supernatural and inward revelation from God, giving a deep consciousness of what I am in *His* sight, which causes me to loathe and condemn myself, resulting in a bitter sorrow for sin, a holy horror and hatred for sin, and a turning away from or forsaking of sin. It is the discovery of God's high and righteous claims upon me, and of my lifelong failure to meet those claims. It is the recognition of the holiness and goodness of His law, and my defiant insubordination thereto. It is the perception that God has the right to rule and govern me, and of my refusal to submit unto Him. It is the apprehension that He has dealt in goodness and kindness with me, and that I have evilly repaid Him by having no concern for *His* honor and glory. It is the realization of His gracious patience with me, and how that instead of this melting my heart and causing me to yield loving obedience to Him, I have *abused* His forebearance by continuing in a course of self-will.

Evangelical repentance is a heart-apprehension of the exceeding sinfulness of sin. It is the recognition of the *chief* thing wherein I am blameworthy, namely, in having so miserably failed to render unto God that which is His rightful due. As the Holy Spirit sets before me the loveliness of the divine character, as I am enabled to discern the exalted excellency of God, then I begin to perceive that to which He is justly entitled, namely, the homage of my heart, the unrestricted love of my soul, the complete surrender of my whole being to Him. As I perceive that from the moment I drew my first breath God has sought *only my good,* that the One who gave me being has constantly ministered to my every creature need, and that the least I can do in return is to acknowledge His abounding mercies by doing that which is pleasing in His sight, I am now overwhelmed with anguish and horror as I realize I have treated Him more vilely than my worst enemy.

Oftentimes example is better than the most accurate definition. The New Testament furnishes quite a number of concrete instances, even where the term itself is not found. When the "publican" stood afar off and would not so much as lift up his eyes unto heaven, but smote upon his breast, saying, "God be merciful to me a sinner" (Luke 18:13), we behold repentance *in action*. He recognized that awful moral distance which sin had taken him from God; he was deeply conscious of his utter unworthiness to gaze upon the Holy One; he unsparingly judged himself; he realized that his only hope lay in the sovereign mercy of God. So, too, the thief on the cross: in his words to his hardened companion, "Dost not thou fear God, seeing thou art in the same *condemnation*, and we indeed *justly;* for we receive the due reward of our deeds" (Luke 23:40-41). There was no self-extenuation, but a ready owning of his sinnership and his desert to be punished.

Mark carefully the expressions of penitence used by David in Psalm 51. He talks not of his "failures," "mistakes" or "infirmities," but instead of "my transgression" (v. 1), "my sin" (v. 2), "this evil" (v. 4), "my iniquity" (v. 9), and expressly mentions the worst feature of his crime, namely, his "bloodguiltiness" (v. 14). True repentance abhors gentle names for sin, nor does it seek to cloak wickedness. That which, while being tempted, is thought of as no great offense, when (later) is truly repented of, is acknowledged to be heinous. Sin before its commission often appears unto the mind as a very small evil, but when grace acts in a way of repentance for it, then the false glamor disappears and it is viewed in its dreadful malignity and loathed accordingly.

True repentance is always accompanied by a deep longing and a sincere determination to forsake that course which is displeasing to God. With what *honesty* could any man seek God's pardon while he continued to defy Him and would not part with that which He forbids? Would any king pardon a traitor, though he seemed ever so humble, if he saw that he would be a traitor still? True, God is infinitely more merciful than any human king, yet in the very passage where He first formally proclaimed His mercy, He at once added, " . . . that will by no means clear the guilty" (Exod. 34:5-7) i.e., the guilty-hearted, those with false and disloyal hearts toward Himself, who would not be subject to Him in all things, and declined to have their every thought brought into captivity to obedience unto Him (II Cor. 10:5).

What has just been said needs to be strongly emphasized in this day of lawlessness, when, on every side, the very "grace of God" is being "turned into lasciviousness" (Jude 4). Many are the Scriptures which set forth this truth, that there must be a *forsaking* of sin before God will pardon offenders. "There is forgiveness with thee, *that* thou mayest be feared" (Ps. 130:4). Were God to grant pardon to those in whom there was no change of heart to fear and obey Him, then there would be mercy with Him that He might be *insulted* and dishonored still further! God's mercy is never exercised at the expense of His holiness! God never displays one of His attributes so as to dishonor another. To pity a thief while he continues his thievery would be folly, not wisdom. Well did the Puritan, T. Goodwin, say, "Resolve either to leave every known sin and submit to every known duty, or else never look to find mercy and favor with God."

Of old it was announced that should any "bless himself in his heart, saying, I shall have peace, though I walk in the imagination of mine heart to add drunkenness to thirst [that is, one sin to another]: the Lord *will not* spare him" (Deut. 28:19-20). So, on the other hand it was declared, "If my people, which are called by my name, shall humble themselves, and pray, and seek *my* face, and *turn from* their wicked ways; *then* will I hear from heaven, and will forgive their sin, and will heal their land" (II Chron. 7:14; cf. 6:26). And the principles of God's government have not changed! The death of Christ has not caused God to *lower* His standard—how unspeakably horrible and dreadful that anyone should suppose it has! No, what God demanded of old, He demands now.

Thus, repentance is the *negative side* of conversion. Conversion is a wholehearted turning unto God, but there cannot be a turning *unto* without a turning *from*. Sin must be forsaken ere we can draw nigh unto the Holy One. As it is written, "Ye turned to God *from idols* to serve [live for] the living and true God" (I Thess. 1:9). Thus, repentance is the sinner *making his peace with God*. We are not unmindful of the fact that that expression is derided by many, yet it is a Scriptural one: "Let him take hold of my strength, that he may make peace with me" (Isa. 27:5). It is blessedly true that *Christ "made peace* through the blood of his cross" (Col. 1:20), yet it is equally true that no sinner ever enters into the saving good of Christ's blood until he makes *his* peace with God; in other words, till he throws down the weapons of his warfare and ceases fighting against God. The Lord Jesus Himself plainly taught this in Luke 14; let the reader *carefully* ponder verses 28-33, paying special attention to verse 32 and the "so likewise" of verse 33!

9 The Implications of Repentance

"If God is an absolutely perfect, an infinitely glorious and amiable Being, infinitely worthy of supreme love and honor, and of universal obedience; and if our disaffection to the divine character and rebellion against God, is altogether inexcusable and infinitely criminal, agreeable to the voice of the divine law, and to the import of the cross of Christ; if God the great Governor of the universe views things in this light, and in this view calls unto us from heaven to confess our sins, repent and turn unto Him with all our hearts; if these things are so—and they are—then the meaning of God's words is certain, the ideas designed to be conveyed by them are determinate. To repent, beyond dispute, is to change our minds as to the divine character, to lay aside our prejudices, to open our eyes, and begin to look upon God as He is, an absolutely perfect, an infinitely glorious and amiable Being, infinitely worthy of supreme love and honor, and of universal obedience; and in the light of this glory to begin to view our disaffection and rebellion as altogether inexcusable and infinitely criminal, and in the view, cordially take all that blame to ourselves which God lays upon us, and to be affected accordingly.

"Repentance is saying, 'Righteous art Thou, O Lord, when Thou speakest, and clear when Thou judgest. Should justice take place, no iniquity should be imputed unto Thee. It would not be a blemish, but a beauty in Thy character, and all heaven ought forever to love and adore Thy glorious majesty, should I receive my just deserts and perish forever. But Thou canst have mercy on whom Thou wilt, through Jesus Christ. To Thine infinite grace and self-moving goodness through Him I look. God be merciful to me a sinner.' Repentance stands, then, in opposition to all our former prejudices against the divine character; and in opposition to that sin-extenuating, self-justifying, law-hating, God-blaming disposition which reigns in every impenitent soul. God is seen in His beauty; the divine law, as a ministration of condemnation and death, appears glorious, our disaffection and rebellion infinitely criminal. We justify God, approve His law, condemn ourselves, accept the punishment of our iniquity as worthy of God; and thus we confess, repent, and turn unto the Lord, looking only to free grace through Jesus Christ for pardon" (Jos. Bellamy, 1750).

A. Repentance, then, presupposes, first, a recognition and *acknowledgment of God's claims* upon us as our Creator, Governor, Provider, and Protector. Because God is who and what He is, namely the Sum and Source of all moral and spiritual excellency, and because of our relation to Him as creatures completely dependent upon Him, He is infinitely entitled to be loved with all our hearts, worshiped with fullest adoration, and served with joyous, perfect, and unremitting obedience. Until there is at least some measure of a clear and definite (we do not say *full*) recognition of this, the mind is yet under the blinding power of Satan (II Cor. 4:4) and the heart is yet alienated from God (Eph. 4:18). Thus, repentance necessarily presupposes *regeneration,* in which the favored soul is "given an understanding that we may know him that is true" (I John 5:20). The first *evidence* that this supernatural enlightenment has been given, is the inward apprehension of God's excellency and supremacy, accompanied by a horrified consciousness of how dreadfully I have failed, all through my life, to give Him His rightful place in my heart and life.

B. In the second place, true repentance presupposes *a hearty approval of God's law* and a full consent to its righteous requirements. "The law is holy, and the commandment is holy, and just, and good" (Rom. 7:12): it cannot be otherwise, for *God* is its Author, and nothing unholy, unjust, or evil, could ever proceed from Him. It therefore follows that *such* a law can never be altered or repealed. Those who affirm that the law of God *has been* abolished, cast the greatest reproach upon all the perfections of the divine character. Upon His *holiness,* whereby He loves the right and hates the wrong: for a repeal of the law would suppose God releasing His creatures from doing right and allowing them to do wrong. Upon His *justice,* whereby He gives to everyone his due: supposing Him to rescind His righteous claims. Upon His *immutability:* supposing Him to have been in one mind in the past, and another in the present. Upon His *goodness:* supposing Him to have canceled that which was designed for our highest well-being.

If the reader will only make a determined effort to grasp the fact that the requirements of God's law are all summed up in "Thou shalt love the Lord thy God with all thine heart . . . " (Deut. 6:5), he ought to have no difficulty in perceiving how frightful is the teaching that the law has been abrogated. Men must indeed have strange conceptions of divine grace and of the gospel, if they suppose that God is now demanding something other or something less than the supreme place in men's affections and lives. Do they think for a moment that in Old Testament times God was asking for more love than was His due? Do they imagine that God does not now deserve as much love as He once did? Such a thought would be the most awful blasphemy. Or, do they suppose that God has relinquished His rights and now freely allows His creatures to despise Him? that He has made a concession to their evil hearts by lowering His standard? Is not the *real* source of opposition to God's law the "enmity of the carnal mind" (Rom. 8:7)?!

Perhaps the reader is inclined to reply, But did not *Christ* come here to fulfill the law for us, and does not *His* obedience *free us* from its demands? Pause, dear friend, and weigh well such a question, and endeavor to see what such a concept plainly involves. Surely you do not mean that the Son of God became incarnate for the purpose of procuring an abatement of the law, or to purchase lawless liberty for His rebellious subjects. What! could He esteem His Father's interest and glory, the honor of His law and government, so lightly? Did He shed His precious blood so as to persuade the great Governor of the world to slacken the reigns of government and grant an impious license to lawlessness? Perish the thought. Such a terrible concept would make the ineffably holy Christ the enemy of God and the friend of sin.

So far from the Son coming to earth for such a purpose, He expressly declared, "Think not that I am come to destroy the law, or the prophets: I am not come to destroy, but to fulfil. For verily I say unto you, Till heaven and earth pass, one jot or one tittle shall in no wise pass from the law, till all be fulfilled" (Matt. 5:17-18). If the verses which follow this quotation be carefully pondered, it will be seen that our Lord denounced the Pharisees because they had, by their own traditions and inventions, nullified God's law: while allowing that it condemned some external and gross acts of sin, they denied that it reprehended the first strivings of corruption in the heart. Therefore did Christ say, "Except your righteousness shall exceed the righteousness of the scribes and Pharisees, ye shall in no case enter into the kingdom of heaven" (Matt. 5:20).

That the law of God was never to be repealed is taught again and again in Psalm 119: "Thy righteousness is an everlasting righteousness and thy law is the truth. . . . The righteousness of thy testimonies is everlasting. . . . Concerning thy testimonies, I have known of old that thou hast founded them forever. . . . Thy Word is true from the beginning, and every one of thy righteous judgments endureth forever" (vv. 142, 144, 152, 160). It was as though the psalmist said, "The duty required by Thy law is right and good, everlastingly right and good; and therefore, as Governor of the world, Thou hast by law forever settled and established it as duty and law never to be altered, but to endure forever and forever; therefore, will it endure."

So far from Christ having died to disannul the law, so that now it wholly ceases to be a rule of life to believers, one great and declared design of His coming into the world was to *recover* His people unto a *conformity thereto* (see Titus 2:11-13). O how men love their corruptions and hate God's law, desiring to have it cashiered so that they may live as they please, and yet escape the reproaches of their consciences here and eternal punishment hereafter. But God "sitteth King for ever" (Ps. 29:10) and will assert the *rights* of His crown, maintain the honor of His majesty and the glory of His great name, and vindicate His injured law. He shall yet say, "But those mine enemies, which would not that I should reign over them, bring hither, and slay before me" (Luke 19:27).

Herein we may see plainly the imperative and absolute *need for regeneration,* if ever a fallen creature is to be won to God and a defiant rebel transformed into a loving subject. "Because the carnal mind is enmity against God; for it is not subject to the law of God, neither indeed can be" (Rom. 8:7)—such is the terrible condition of every man and woman by nature. Nothing but the supernatural operation of the almighty Spirit of God can produce a change of heart, so that one can truthfully say, "I *delight* in the *law* of God after the inward man" (Rom. 7:22). But such teaching as this never has been and never will be popular in the world. The false prophets who cry, "Peace, peace," will be loved, but they who press the high and unchanging claims of a righteous God will be hated and denounced as "legalists," and much more.

Christ came into this world and died to answer all the demands of the law, and this, not only that sinners might be saved, but that the law itself might be the more firmly "established," i.e., in the consciences and hearts of the redeemed. Therefore did the apostle write, "Do we then make void the law through faith? God forbid: yea, we establish the law" (Rom. 3:31). In this very Epistle of the Romans the apostle, moved by the Holy Spirit, lays it down as a first principle that "the wrath of God is revealed from heaven against all ungodliness and unrighteousness of men who hold the truth in unrighteousness" (Rom. 1:18). From this premise, he goes on to prove that "now we know that what thing soever the law saith, it saith to them who are under the law: *that* every mouth may be stopped, and all the world may become guilty before God" (3:19). But is it not clear as a sunbeam that if the law had been repealed at the cross that none *could* stand "guilty" before God, for "sin is not imputed when there is no law" (Rom. 5:13)!

If the law were repealed, what need was there for such a long train of argument to prove that "by the deeds of the law there shall no flesh be justified in his sight" (3:20)? In such case, it had been quite sufficient to say that a repealed law could neither justify nor condemn anybody. Instead, the apostle shows that the law requires a "patient continuance in well doing" and threatens "tribulation and anguish upon every soul of man that doeth evil" (Rom. 2:5, 7). This shows that both Jews and Gentiles have sinned and, therefore, are condemned by the law—brought in guilty— and so the apostle draws the inevitable conclusion that none can be cleared or justified by the law. Is it not obvious, then, that all this inspired reasoning supposes that the law is as much enforced as ever? Accordingly he goes on to show Christ's death answered the demands of the law, and that, *not* to make it void, but to *"establish"* it.

Hence it is that we find the New Testament Scriptures uniformly speak of those who have no saving interest in Christ's righteousness by faith, as being as much under the wrath of God and the curse of the law as though He had never died. As we have seen, Romans 1:18 declares, "The wrath of God is [not "was"] revealed from heaven against *all* ungodliness and unrighteousness of men." Again, in Galatians 3:10 we are told, "For as many as are of the works of the law *are* under the curse: for it is written: Cursed is every one that continueth not in *all* things which are written in the book of the law to do them" (compare II Thess. 1:7-9). But if the law had been repealed by the death of Christ, then all the world would have been *freed* from the curse, for a repealed law can neither bless the righteous nor curse the wicked!

Therefore it is we find that when Christless sinners are *really* awakened by the Holy Spirit to see and feel what a dreadful state they are in, they are always convinced that *they are under* the wrath of God and the curse of His law: see Romans 7:9-11, and thereby are they made to understand their dire need of a Saviour. But how could the Holy Spirit *use* the law if it had been repealed? And what of those who are never awakened and convicted by the Spirit, and who continue to despise the claims of God and flout His holy law? Ah, they shall find that after their hardness and impenitent heart they have but treasured up unto themselves "wrath against the day of wrath and revelation of the righteous judgment of God" (Rom. 2:5).

God the Father, as the Governor of the world, *gave* the law. God the Son *magnified* it (Isa. 42:21) by expounding its purity, by obeying its precepts, by enduring its penalty. God the Holy Spirit honors the law by pressing upon the *sinner* its holy demands, and using it as a "schoolmaster" to bring him to Christ (Gal. 3:24). It is the special work of the Third Person of the Trinity to communicate unto each of the elect a sense of the infinite glory of God, the equity of His law, and the righteousness of His claims upon them. He begets within them a disposition which conforms them unto the discharge of their duties, and this He does by putting the *law* into their minds and writing it in their hearts (Heb. 8:10). In this way it becomes their very nature to *love* God with all their heart so that they "might serve him without (servile) fear in holiness and righteousness before him, all the days of our life" (Luke 1:74-75). Thus do both the Son and the Spirit honor the Father as Supreme Govenor, and join in the same design to discountenance sin, humble the sinner, magnify the law, and glorify grace.

But this enforcing of the infinite glory of God, of His governmental supremacy, of His holy law, of His righteous claims, of His demand for loving obedience and an implicit compliance with all His commands, is what is *left out* of every false religion in the world. And today there are, perhaps, as many false religions *inside* of Christendom as there are outside—denials of the Truth, perversions of the Truth, half-truths twisted and mangled, lawlessness proclaimed under the pretense of exalting grace. "Pretense" we say, for God's grace never reigns at the expense of righteousness but "through righteousness" (Rom. 5:21). Divine grace teaches us that "denying ungodliness and worldly lusts, we should live soberly, righteously, and godly, in this present world" (Titus 2:13). It is the ministers of Satan, "deceitful workers" (II Cor. 11:13), who are now by their one-sided teaching causing many to "turn the grace of our God into lasciviousness" (Jude 4).

Here, then, is the explanation why true repentance is so little preached today. The sense of God's governmental supremacy has been lost, the claims of His righteousness are ignored, the unchanging demands of His holy law are no longer recognized, hence, the unregenerate, not knowing God, having no sense of His infinite glory, and there being practically nothing in present-day preaching to instruct them therein, it follows that all their fancied reverence for and devotion to God takes its rise from merely *selfish* considerations, nothing but self-love (the *natural* instinct of self-preservation) lying at the bottom of modern "Christianity." As it is natural for unregenerate men to suppose they deserve something for their duties, so it is natural for them to be insensible of the infinite evil of their sins. And hence it is that new gospels are invented, new notions of "the way of salvation" are contrived, to *suit* the depraved taste of unhumbled and impenitent sinners, who are concerned about *their own* interests and care not what becomes of God's glory.

C. In the third place, true repentance presupposes a frank and *broken-hearted acknowledgment of our wicked failure* to keep God's righteous law. When the Holy Spirit opens the eyes of a sinner to see, in some measure, the supreme excellency and loveliness of the divine character, and shows him how infinitely worthy God is of our sincere adoration: when He assures us of the righteousness and goodness of God's law, and how justly He is entitled to be loved by us with *all* our hearts; and when He convicts us of our wretched and lifelong failure to respond unto His most just claims upon us; when He makes us feel that so far from having delighted ourselves in this infinitely glorious God, we have sought to dismiss Him from our thoughts, and set our hearts upon the perishing things of time and sense, seeking our satisfaction in *them;* and that so far from having owned His rightful supremacy over us and His just claim for our lives to be governed by Him, we have scorned His authority, ignored His commandments, and acted only in self-will—then it is, for the first time, we begin to *perceive* the infinite evil of sin, and are filled with self-loathing, horror, and grief at our terrible course of conduct.

What we have just endeavored to set forth is as different from what the strivings of an uneasy conscience produces as light is from darkness. One who has never been the subject of the supernatural and gracious operations of the Spirit may blame himself for sabbath-breaking, taking the Lord's name in vain, lying, drunkenness, who has never felt himself to blame for being disaffected to the divine character. Even the wicked king Saul once acknowledged, "I have sinned, I have played the fool, and have erred exceedingly" (I Sam. 26:21). So has many another since then, who was yet altogether blind to *the chief thing* wherein he was to blame. While men are ignorant of the beauty of God's character, of how absolutely worthy He is of being loved; while they perceive not the equity and blessedness of His law, of how absolutely entitled it is to implicit, unremitting, and joyous obedience; it is impossible that they should *repent* because of their failure to render *this* to Him.

Just as the absence of love to God, together with disaffection to His holy character, lies at the root of and influences the whole course of wickedness which mankind generally live in, so when Scripture calls upon men to repent of particular sins and turn to God, it is their *lack of love* for God and their *enmity against* His law, as manifested in and by their particular sins, which they are required to repent of. There is no sin whatsoever that any man is guilty of, but what it proceeds from a disrespect of God's character and a disregard of His authority. Thus it was said of David's sin that he not only had "despised the commandment of the Lord," but had "despised me," the Lord (II Sam. 12:9-10). Therefore in repentance we are required not only to judge our particular sins, but also that *insubordination to God* which produced them: we are to unsparingly and bitterly condemn ourselves because we have treated the Lord of glory, the King of the universe, with contempt. *That* is *the* crime for which we are, above all things else, to blame. Not until we have realized that our rebellion against God was *such* that nothing but the *death of Christ* could possibly atone for it, have we truly repented.

Thus, genuine and saving repentance is a taking sides with God *against myself*. It is *not* that our repentance expiates our sins, for there is nothing meritorious about it. It makes *no* amends for our past vile conduct, nor does it move God to mercy. Yet is repentance required, yea demanded of us, and divine mercy is not shown where no repentance is. No, repentance is designed to make the heart *loathe* sin, and that through a deep sense of its infinite enormity and dreadful pollution; it is to make us *dread* sin through a heart-realization of its awful guilt. Only thus is the stubborn will broken and the heart made contrite and prepared to turn unto the Lord Jesus and seek salvation through Him by grace alone.

D. *There are three kinds of repentance spoken of in Scripture.* First, that of desperation: Esau, Pharaoh, Ahithophel, and Judas are illustrations. Second, that of reformation: Ahab's and that which was brought about under the preaching of Jonah, are illustrations. Third, that which is unto salvation: Acts 11:18; II Corinthians 7:10. It is most important that we learn to discriminate between legal conviction and evangelical repentance. Multitudes are deceived at this point: they suppose that because they have been terrified through contemplating the wrath to come and have abandoned many of their evil ways, they have repented. This by no means follows. A legal conviction fears *hell,* evangelical repentance reveres *God:* the one dreads *punishment,* the other hates *sin;* the one informs the mind, the other melts the heart. Evangelical repentance makes no excuses and has no reserves, but cries, "I have dishonored Thy name, grieved Thy Spirit, abused Thy patience."

When a sinner is brought to truly realize that he is in great danger, he earnestly desires and diligently seeks deliverance, but that is from the natural instinct of self-preservation, and not because of supernatural grace at work in his heart. Tell him that *nothing* is required from him except to believe in Christ, rest on His finished work, and like a stony-ground hearer he at once receives the Word with joy, and no human being can make him doubt his salvation. Yet his heart has never been broken before God, nor has he any true love for Him. Such people mend their ways and become quite zealous religionists. They pray earnestly, read the Bible frequently, and sometimes become active workers in warning their fellows. But tell such that notwithstanding their tears, zeal, and believing the letter of Scripture, they deserve to be damned as much as ever they did, and that God can justly *refuse* them mercy, and their enmity against Him is likely to become swiftly apparent.

Thousands of deceived souls in Christendom, deluded by the false gospellers of the day, love a God who has no existence except in their own disordered imaginations. And terrible beyond words will be their disillusionment in the next world. "How sad and dreadful a thing will it be for such poor sinners when they come to die, and enter into the world of spirits, there to find that the God they once loved and trusted in, was nothing but an image framed in their own fancy! They hated the God *of Scripture,* and hated His *law,* and therefore would not believe that either God or His law were indeed what they were. They were resolved to have a god and a law more to their own minds. How dreadful will their disappointment be! How terrible their surprise! They would never own that *they* were enemies to God; now they will see that their enmity was so great as to make them resolutely—notwithstanding the plainest evidence— even to deny Him to be what He was. And how righteous will the ways of the Lord appear to be unto them then, in that He gave such over to strong delusion to believe a lie, because they would not love nor believe the truth, but had pleasure in unrighteousness" (Jos. Bellamy).

While God be considered *merely* as creditor and sinners as debtors and Christ is regarded as paying the *whole* debt of all who believe, it cannot but be that souls will be fatally misled. Because Christ obeyed the law as well as suffered its penalty, it by no means follows that we are discharged from doing our duty. Yet, it is now being taught on every side that Christ has done all, and that there is nothing to do but firmly believe in Him, that Christians have nothing to do with the law—no, not as a rule of life—that they have been freed from all obligations to any duty. But Scripture affirms that Christ died to "purify unto himself a peculiar people, zealous of good works" (Titus 2:14), and that so far from the Christian being discharged from duty, his obligations are immeasurably increased by the grace of the gospel (Rom. 12:1). But everything is viewed in a false light today, and instead of Christ being regarded as the Friend of *holiness*, He is made the Minister of *sin*.

"Repentance to be sure must be *entire*. Many will say, Sir, I will re- nounce this sin and the other, but there are certain darling lusts which I must keep. O sirs, in God's name let me intreat you: it is not the giving up of any one sin, nor fifty sins, which is true repentance; it is the solemn renunciation of *every* sin. If thou dost harbor one of these accursed vipers in thy heart, thy repentance is but a sham, if thou dost indulge in but one lust, and dost give up every other, that one lust, like one leak in a ship, will sink the soul. Think it not sufficient to give up thy outward vices, fancy it not enough to cut off the more corrupt sins of thy life; it is all or none which God demands. 'Repent,' says He, and when He bids you *repent*, He means repent of all thy sins, otherwise He can never accept thy repentance as being real. He says, 'Gild thee as thou wilt, O sinner, I abhor thee! Aye, make thyself gaudy, like the snake in its azure scales, I hate thee still, for I know thy venom, and I will flee from thee when thou comest to Me in thy most specious garb. All sin must be given up, or else you shall never have Christ; all transgression must be renounced, or else the gates of heaven must be barred against thee. Let us remember this, that repentance to be sincere, it must be *entire*.

"True repentance is a turning of *the heart*, as well as of the life, it is the giving up of the whole soul to God, to be His forever and ever; it is a renunciation of the sins of the heart, as well as of the crimes of the life. Let none of us fancy we have repented, when we have only a false and fictitious repentance; let none of us take that to be the work of the Spirit, which is only the work of poor human nature; let us not dream that we have savingly turned to God, when perhaps we have only turned to ourselves, let us not think it enough to have turned from vice to virtue; let us remember it must be a turning of the whole soul to God, so as to be made anew in Christ Jesus; otherwise we have not met the requirements of the text.

"Lastly, upon this point, true repentance must be *perpetual.* It is not my turning to God during today that will be a proof I am a true convert; it is forsaking my sins throughout the entire course of my life, until I sleep in the grave. You must not fancy that to be upright for a week will be a proof that you are saved, it is a perpetual abhorrence of evil. The change which *God* works is neither a transitory nor superficial one; not a cutting off the top of the weed, but an eradication of it; not the sweeping away of the dust of one day, but the taking away of that which is the cause of the dust. You may today go home and pretend to pray, you may today be serious, tomorrow honest, and the next day you may pretend to be devout; but yet, if you *return*—as Scripture has it, like the dog to its vomit and like the sow to its wallowing in the mire—your repentance shall but sink you deeper into hell, instead of being a proof of divine grace in your heart" (from Spurgeon's sermon on Psalm 7:12). Would that such faithful sermons were being preached in the so-called orthodox and "fundamentalist" pulpits today.

"To learn *by* heart that which others say *from* the heart—to get the outline of a believer's experience, and then to adopt it skillfully to one's self as our *own* experience—this is a thing so simple, that instead of wondering there are hypocrites, I often marvel that there are not ten times more. And then again, the graces—the real graces within—are very easy to counterfeit. There is a repentance that needs to be repented of, and yet it approaches near as possible to true repentance. Does repentance make men hate sin? they who have a false repentance may detest some crimes. Does repentance make men resolve that they will not sin? so will this false repentance, for Balaam said, 'If Balak would give me his house full of silver and gold, I will not go beyond the word of the Lord.' Does true repentance make men humble themselves? so does false repentance, for Ahab humbled himself before God, and yet perished. There is a line of distinction so fine that an eagle's eye hath not seen it; and only God Himself, and the soul that is enlightened by His Spirit, can tell whether our repentance be real or no" (Spurgeon on Luke 13:24).

10 The Fruits of Repentance

To help the exercised reader identify true repentance, consider the fruits that demonstrate godly repentance.

A. *A real hatred of sin as sin, not merely its consequences.* A hatred not only of this or that sin, but of all sin, and particularly of the root itself: self-will. "Thus saith the Lord God, Repent, and turn from your idols; and turn away your faces from all your abominations" (Ezek. 14:6). He who hates not sin, loves it. God's demand is, "Ye shall loathe yourselves in your own sight for all your evils that ye have committed" (Ezek. 20:43). One who has really repented can truthfully say, "I hate every false way" (Ps. 119:104). He who once thought a course of holy living was a gloomy thing, has another judgment now. He who once regarded a course of self-pleasing as attractive, now detests it and has purposed to forsake all sin forever. This is the change of mind which God requires.

B. *A deep sorrow for sin.* The nonsaving repentance of so many is principally a distress occasioned by forebodings of divine wrath; but evangelical repentance produces a deep grief from a sense of having offended so infinitely excellent and glorious a Being as God. The one is the effect of fear, the other of love; the one is only for a brief season, the other is the habitual practice for life. Many a man is filled with regret and remorse over a misspent life, yet has no poignant sorrow of heart for his ingratitude and rebellion against God. But a regenerated soul is cut to the quick for having disregarded and opposed his great Benefactor and rightful Sovereign. This is the change of heart which God requires.

"Ye sorrowed to repentance: for ye were made sorry after a godly manner . . . for godly sorrow worketh repentance to salvation" (II Cor. 7:9-10). Such a sorrow is produced in the heart by the Holy Spirit and has God for its object. It is a grief for having despised *such* a God, rebelled against *His* authority, and been indifferent to *His* glory. It is this which causes us to "weep bitterly" (Matt. 26:75). He who has not grieved over sin takes pleasure therein. God requires us to "afflict" our souls (Lev. 16:29). His call is, "Turn ye even to me with all your heart, and with fasting, and with weeping, and with mourning: and rend your hearts and not your garments, and turn unto the Lord your God: for he is gracious and merciful" (Joel 2:12-13). Only that sorrow for sin is genuine which causes us to crucify "the flesh with the affections and lusts" (Gal. 5:24).

C. *A confessing of sin.* "He that covereth his sins shall not prosper" (Prov. 28:13). It is "second nature" to the sinner to *deny* his sins, directly or indirectly, to minimize, or make excuses for them. It was thus with Adam and Eve at the beginning. But when the Holy Spirit works in any soul, his sins are brought to light, and he, in turn, acknowledges them to God. There is no relief for the stricken heart until he does so: "When I kept silence, my bones waxed old through my roaring all the day long, for day and night thy hand was heavy upon me: my moisture is turned into the drought of summer" (Ps. 32:3-4). The frank and brokenhearted owning of our sins is imperative if peace of conscience is to be maintained. This is the change of attitude which God requires.

D. *An actual turning from sin.* "Surely there is no one here so stupefied with the laudanum of hellish indifference as to imagine that he can revel in his lusts, and afterward wear the white robes of the redeemed in Paradise. If you imagine you can be partakers of the blood of Christ, and yet drink the cup of Belial; if you imagine you can be members of Satan and members of Christ at the same time, ye have less sense than one would give you credit for. No, you know that right hands must be cut off and right eyes plucked out—that the most darling sins must be renounced—if you would enter the kingdom of God" (from Spurgeon on Luke 13:24).

Three Greek words are used in the New Testament which present different phases of repentance. First, *metanoeo,* which means a change of mind (Matt. 3:2; Mark 1:15, etc.). Second, *metanolomai,* which means a change of heart (Matt. 21:29, 32; Heb. 7:21, etc.). Third, *metanoia,* which means a change of course or life (Matt. 3:8; 9:13; Acts 20:21). The three must go together for a genuine repentance. Many experience a change of mind: they are instructed, and know better, but they continue to defy God. Some are even exercised in heart or conscience, yet they continue in sin. Some amend their ways, yet not from love to God and hatred of sin. Some are informed in mind and uneasy in heart, who never reform their lives. The three *must* go together.

"He that covereth his sins shall not prosper, but whoso confesseth and *forsaketh* them shall have mercy" (Prov. 28:13). He who does not, fully in his heart's desire and increasingly so in his life, turn from his wicked ways has not repented. If I really hate sin and sorrow over it, shall I not abandon it? Note carefully the "wherein in time *past*" of Ephesians 2:2 and "*were* sometimes" of Titus 3:3! "Let the *wicked forsake* his way, and the unrighteous man his thoughts, and let him return unto the Lord, and he will have mercy upon him" (Isa. 55:7). This is the change, of course, which God requires.

E. *Accompanied by restitution where this is necessary and possible.* No repentance can be true which is not accompanied by a *complete* amendment of life. The prayer of a genuinely penitent soul is, "Create in me a clean heart, O God, and renew a right spirit within me" (Ps. 51:10). And where one really desires to be right with God, he does so with his fellowmen too. One who, in his past life, has wronged another, and now makes no determined effort to do everything in his power to right that wrong, certainly has not repented! John G. Paton tells of how after a certain servant was converted, the first thing he did was to restore unto his master all the articles which he had stolen from him!

F. *These fruits are permanent.* Because true repentance is preceded by a realization of the loveliness and excellency of the divine character and an apprehension of the exceeding sinfulness of sin for having treated with contempt so infinitely glorious a Being, contrition for and hatred of all evil is abiding. As we grow in grace and in the knowledge of the Lord, of our indebtedness and obligations to Him, our repentance deepens, we judge ourselves more thoroughly, and take a lower and lower place before Him. The more the heart pants after a closer walk with God, the more will it put away everything which hinders this.

G. *Yet repentance is never perfect in this life.* Our faith is never so complete that we get to the place where the heart is no more harassed with doubtings. And our repentance is never so pure that it is altogether free from hardness of heart. Repentance is a lifelong act. We need to pray daily for a deeper repentance.

In view of all that has been said, we trust it is now abundantly clear to every impartial reader that those preachers who *repudiate* repentance are, to poor lost souls, "physicians of *no* value." They who leave out repentance, are preaching "another gospel" (Gal. 1:6) than Christ (Mark 1:15; 6:12) and His apostles (Acts 17:30; 20:21) proclaimed. Repentance is an evangelical duty, though it is not to be rested in, for it contributes *nothing* unto salvation. Those who have never repented are yet in the snare of the devil (II Tim. 2:25-26), and are treasuring up to themselves wrath against the day of wrath (Rom. 2:4-5).

"If, therefore, sinners would take the wisest course to be the better for the use of the means of grace, they must try to fall in with God's design and the Spirit's influences, and labor to see and feel their sinful, guilty, undone state. For this end they must forsake vain company, drop their inordinate worldly pursuits, abandon everything which tends to keep them secure in sin and quench the motions of the Spirit; and for this end must they read, meditate, and pray; comparing themselves with God's holy law, trying to view themselves in the same light that God does, and pass the same judgment upon themselves; so that they may be in a way to approve of the law and admire the grace of the gospel; to judge themselves and humbly apply to the free grace of God through Jesus Christ for all things, and return through Him to God" (Jos. Bellamy).

A summary of what has been before us may be helpful to some. 1. Repentance is an evangelical duty, and no preacher is entitled to be regarded as a servant of Christ's if he be silent thereon (Luke 24:47). 2. Repentance is required by God in this dispensation (Acts 17:30) as in all preceding ones. 3. Repentance is in nowise meritorious, yet without it the gospel cannot be savingly believed (Matt. 21:32; Mark 1:15). 4. Repentance is a Spirit-given realization of the exceeding sinfulness of sin and a taking sides with God against myself. 5. Repentance presupposes a hearty approval of God's law and a full consent to its righteous requirements, which are all summed up in "Thou shalt love the Lord thy God with all thy heart. . . ." 6. Repentance is accompanied by a genuine hatred of and sorrow for sin. 7. Repentance is evidenced by a forsaking of sin. 8. Repentance is known by its permanency: there must be a continual turning away from sin and grieving over each fall thereinto. 9. Repentance, while permanent, is never complete or perfect in this life. 10. Repentance is to be sought as a gift of Christ (Acts 5:31).

PART THREE
Coming to Christ

11 Introduction

By way of introduction let us bring before the readers the following Scriptures. (1) "Ye will not come to me, that ye might have life" (John 5:40). (2) "Come unto me, all ye that labour and are heavy laden, and I will give you rest" (Matt. 11:28). (3) "No man can come to me, except the Father which hath sent me draw him" (John 6:44). (4) "All that the Father giveth me shall come to me; and him that cometh to me I will in no wise cast out" (John 6:37). (5) "If any man come to me, and hate not his father, and mother, and wife, and children, and brethren, and sisters, yea, and his own life also, he cannot be my disciple. And whosoever doth not bear his cross, and come after me, cannot be my disciple" (Luke 14:26-27). (6) "To whom coming, as unto a living stone, disallowed indeed of men, but chosen of God, and precious" (I Peter 2:4). (7) "Wherefore he is able also to save them to the uttermost that come unto God by him, seeing he ever liveth to make intercession for them" (Heb. 7:25).

The first of these passages applies to every unregenerate man and woman on this earth. While he is in a state of nature, no man can come to Christ. Though all excellencies both divine and human are found in the Lord Jesus, though He is "altogether lovely" (Song of Sol. 5:16), yet the fallen sons of Adam see in Him "no beauty that [they] should desire him" (Isa. 53:2). They may be well instructed in "the doctrine of Christ," they may believe unhesitatingly all that Scripture affirms concerning Him, they may frequently take His name upon their lips, profess to be resting on His finished work, sing His praises, yet their hearts are far from Him. The things of this world have the first place in their affections. The gratifying of self is their dominant concern. They surrender not their lives to Him. He is too holy to suit their love of sin; His claims are too exacting to suit their selfish hearts; His terms of discipleship are too severe to suit their fleshly ways. They will not yield to His lordship—true alike with each one of us till God performs a miracle of grace upon our hearts.

The second passage contains a gracious invitation, made by the compassionate Saviour to a particular class of sinners. The "all" is at once qualified, clearly and definitely, by the words which immediately follow it. The character of those to whom this loving word belongs is clearly defined: it is those who "labour" and are "heavy laden." Most clearly, then, it applies not to the vast majority of our light-hearted, gay-hearted, pleasure-seeking fellows, who have no regard for God's glory and no concern about their eternal welfare. No, the word for such poor creatures is rather, "Rejoice, O young man, in thy youth; and let thy heart cheer thee in the days of thy youth, and walk in the ways of thine heart, and in the sight of thine eyes; but know thou, for all these things God *will* bring thee into judgment" (Eccles. 11:9). But to those who have "laboured" hard to keep the law and please God, who are "heavy laden" with a felt sense of their utter inability to meet His requirements and who long to be delivered from the power and pollution of sin, Christ says, "Come unto me, and I will give you rest."

The third passage quoted above at once tells us that "coming to Christ" is not the easy matter so many imagine it, nor so simple a thing as most preachers represent it to be. Instead of its so being, the incarnate Son of God positively declares that such an act is utterly impossible to a fallen and depraved creature unless and until divine power is brought to bear upon him. A most pride-humbling, flesh-withering, man-abasing word is this. "Coming to Christ" is a far, far different thing from raising your hand to be prayed for by some Protestant "priest," coming forward and taking some cheap-jack evangelist's hand, signing some "decision" card, uniting with some "church," or any other of the "many inventions" (Eccles. 7:29) of man. Before anyone can or will "come to Christ" the understanding must be enlightened, the heart must be supernaturally changed, the stubborn will must be supernaturally broken.

The fourth passage is also one that is unpalatable to the carnal mind, yet is it a precious portion unto the Spirit-taught children of God. It sets forth the blessed truth of unconditional election, or the discriminating grace of God. It speaks of a favored people whom the Father gives to His Son. It declares that everyone of that blessed company shall come to Christ; neither the effects of their fall in Adam, the power of indwelling sin, the hatred and untiring efforts of Satan, nor the deceptive delusions of blind preachers, will be able finally to hinder them—when God's appointed hour arrives, each of His elect is delivered from the power and darkness and is translated into the kingdom of His dear Son. It announces that each such one who comes to Christ, no matter how unworthy and vile he be in himself, no matter how black and long the awful catalog of his sins, He will by no means despise or fail to welcome him, and under no circumstances will He ever cast him off.

The fifth passage is one that makes known the terms on which alone Christ is willing to receive sinners. Here the uncompromising claims of His holiness are set out. He must be crowned Lord of all, or He will not be Lord at all. There must be the complete heart-renunciation of all that stands in competition with Him. He will brook no rival. All that pertains to "the flesh," whether found in a loved one or in self, has to be hated. The "cross" is the badge of Christian discipleship: not a golden one worn on the body, but the principle of self-denial and self-sacrifice ruling the heart. How evident is it, then, that a mighty, supernatural, divine work of grace *must* be wrought in the human heart if any man will even *desire* to meet such terms!

The sixth passage tells us that the Christian is to *continue as he began*. We are to "come to Christ" not once and for all, but frequently, daily. He is the only One who can minister to our needs, and to Him we must constantly turn. In our felt emptiness, we must draw from His fullness (John 1:16). In our weakness, we must turn to Him for strength. In our ignorance we must apply to Him for wisdom. In our falls into sin we must seek afresh His cleansing. *All* that we need for time and eternity is stored up in Him; refreshment when we are weary (Isa. 40:31), healing of body when we are sick (Exod. 15:26), comfort when we are sad (I Peter 5:7), deliverance when we are tempted (Heb. 2:18). If we have wandered away from Him, left our first love, then the remedy is to "repent, and do the first works" (Rev. 2:5); that is, cast ourselves upon Him anew, come just as we did the first time we came to Him—as unworthy, self-confessed sinners, seeking His mercy and forgiveness.

The seventh passage assures us of the eternal security of those who do come. Christ saves "unto the uttermost" or "for evermore" those who come unto God by Him. He is not of one mind today and of another tomorrow. No, He is "the same yesterday, and today, and for ever" (Heb. 13:8). "Having loved his own which were in the world, he loved them unto the end" (John 13:1), and "He ever liveth to make intercession for them." Inasmuch as *His* prayers are effectual, for He declares that the Father hears Him "always" (John 11:42), none whose name is indelibly stamped on the heart of our great High Priest can ever perish. Hallelujah!

12 Obstacles to Coming to Christ

A. *The natural man is unable to "come to Christ."* Let us quote John 6:44: "No man can come to me, except the Father which hath sent me draw him." The reason why this is such a "hard saying," even unto thousands who profess to be Christians, is that they utterly fail to realize the terrible havoc which the Fall has wrought; and, it is greatly to be feared, because they are themselves strangers to "the plague" of their own hearts (I Kings 8:28). Surely if the Spirit had ever awakened them from the sleep of spiritual death, and given them to see something of the dreadful state they were in by nature, and they had been brought to feel that the carnal mind *in them* was "enmity against God" (Rom. 8:7), then they would no longer cavil against this solemn word of Christ's. But the spiritually dead can neither see nor feel spiritually.

Wherein lies the total inability of the natural man? It is *not in the lack of the necessary faculties.* This needs to be plainly insisted upon, otherwise fallen man would cease to be a responsible creature. Fearful as were the effects of the Fall, they deprived man of none of the faculties with which God originally endowed him. True it is that the coming of sin took away from man all power to use those faculties aright, that is to employ them for the glory of his Maker. Nevertheless, fallen man possesses identically the same threefold nature, of spirit and soul and body, as he did before the Fall. No part of man's being was annihilated, though each part was defiled and corrupted by sin. True, man died spiritually, but death is not extinction of being: spiritual death is *alienation from God* (Eph. 4:18): the spiritually dead one is very much alive and active in the service of Satan.

No, the inability of fallen man to "come to Christ" lies in no physical or mental defect. He has the same feet to take him unto a place where the gospel is preached as he has to walk with to a tavern. He has the same eyes with which to read the Holy Scriptures as he has to read the world's newspapers. He has the same lips and voice for calling upon God as he now uses in idle talk or foolish song. So, too, he has the same mental faculties for pondering the things of God and the concerns of eternity as he now uses so diligently in connection with his business. It is because of this that man is "without excuse." It is the *misuse* of the faculties with which the Creator has endowed him that increases man's guilt. Let every servant of God see to it that these things are constantly pressed upon his unsaved hearers.

B. *Man's inability lies in his corrupt nature.* We have to search deeper in order to find the seat of man's spiritual impotency. Through Adam's fall, and through our own sin, our nature has become so debased and depraved that it is impossible for any man to "come to Christ," to "love Him and serve Him," to esteem Him more highly than all the world put together and submit to His rule, until the Spirit of God renews him and implants a new nature. A bitter fountain cannot send forth sweet waters, nor an evil tree produce good fruit. Let us try to make this still clearer by an illustration. It is the *nature* of a vulture to feed upon carrion; true, it has the same bodily members to feed upon the wholesome grain the hens do, but it lacks the disposition and relish for it. It is the nature of a sow to wallow in the mire; true, it has the same legs as a sheep to conduct it to the meadow, but it lacks the desire for the green pastures. So it is with unregenerate man. He has the same physical and mental faculties as the regenerate have for the things and service of God, but he has no love for them.

"Adam . . . begat a son in his own likeness, after his image" (Gen. 5:3). What an awful contrast is found here with that which we read two verses before: "God created man, in the likeness of God made he him." In the interval, Adam had fallen, and a fallen parent could beget only a fallen child, transmitting unto him his own depravity. "Who can bring a clean thing out of an unclean?" (Job 14:4). Therefore do we find the sweet singer of Israel declaring, "Behold, I was shapen in iniquity; and in sin did my mother conceive me" (Ps. 51:5). Though, later, grace made him the man after God's own heart, yet by nature David (as we) was a mass of iniquity and sin. How early does this corruption of nature appear in children. "Even a child is known by his doings" (Prov. 20:11)—the evil bias of its heart is soon manifested: pride, self-will, vanity, lying, averseness to good, are the bitter fruits which quickly appear on the tender but vitiated twig.

C. *Man's inability lies in the complete darkness of his understanding.* This leading faculty of the soul has been despoiled of its primitive glory, and covered over with confusion. Both mind and conscience are defiled: "There is none that understandeth" (Rom. 3:11). Solemnly did the apostle remind the saints, "Ye were sometimes darkness" (Eph. 5:8), not merely "in darkness" but "darkness" itself. "Sin has closed the windows of the soul, darkness is over all the region: it is the land of darkness and shadow of death, where the light is as darkness. The prince of darkness reigns there, and nothing but the works of darkness are framed there. We are born spiritually blind, and cannot be restored without a miracle of grace. This is thy case whoever thou art, that art not born again" (Thos. Boston, 1680). "They are wise to do evil, but to do good they have no knowledge" (Jer. 4:22).

"The carnal mind is enmity against God: for it is not subject to the law of God, neither indeed can be" (Rom. 8:7). There is in the unregenerate *an opposition* to spiritual things and an aversion against them. God has made a revelation of His will unto sinners touching the way of salvation, yet they will not walk therein. They hear that Christ alone is able to save, yet they refuse to part with those things that hinder their coming to Him. They hear that it is sin which slays the soul, and yet they cherish it in their bosoms. They heed not the threatenings of God. Men believe that fire will burn them, and are at great pains to avoid it; yet they show by their actions that they regard the everlasting burnings as a mere scarecrow. The divine commandments are "holy, just and good," but men hate them, and observe them only so far as their respectability among men is promoted.

D. *His inability lies in the complete corruption of his affections.* "Man as he is, before he receives the grace of God, loves anything and everything above spiritual things. If you want proof of this, look around you. There needs no monument to the depravity of the human affections. Cast your eyes everywhere—there is not a street, nor a house, nay, nor a heart, which doth nor bear upon it sad evidence of this dreadful truth. Why is it that men are not found on the Sabbath day universally flocking to the house of God? Why are we not more constantly found reading our Bibles? How is it that prayer is a duty almost universally neglected? Why is Christ Jesus so little beloved? Why are even His professed followers so cold in their affections to Him? Whence arise these things? Assuredly, dear brethren, we can trace them to no other source than this, the corruption and vitiation of the affections. We love that which we ought to hate, and we hate that which we ought to love. It is but human nature, fallen human nature, that man should love this present life better than the life to come. It is but the effect of the fall, that man should love sin better than righteousness, and the way of this world better than the ways of God." (C. H. Spurgeon, sermon on John 6:44).

The affections of the unrenewed man are wholly depraved and distempered. "The heart is deceitful above all things, and *desperately wicked*" (Jer. 17:9). Solemnly did the Lord Jesus affirm that the affections of fallen man are a mother of abominations: "For from within [not from the devil], out of the heart of men, proceed evil thoughts, adulteries, fornications, murders, thefts, covetousness, wickedness, deceit, lasciviousness, an evil eye, blasphemy, pride, foolishness" (Mark 7:21-22). The natural man's affections are wretchedly misplaced; he is a spiritual monster. His heart is where his feet should be, fixed on the earth; his heels are lifted up against heaven, which his heart should be set on (Acts 9:5). His face is toward hell, his back toward heaven; and therefore God calls to him to turn. He joys in what he ought to mourn for, and mourns for what he should rejoice in; glories in his shame, and is ashamed of his glory; abhors what he should desire, and desires what he should abhor (Prov. 2:13-15) (from Boston's *Fourfold State*).

E. *His inability lies in the total perversity of his will.* "Oh," said the Arminian, "men may be saved if they will." We reply, " 'My dear sir, we all believe that; but it is just the *if they will* that is the difficulty.' We assert that no man *will* come to Christ unless he be drawn; nay, *we* do not assert it, but *Christ* Himself declares it: 'Ye will not come unto me that ye might have life' (John 5:40); and as long as that 'ye will not come' stands on record in Holy Scripture, we shall not be brought to believe in any doctrine of the freedom of the human will. It is strange how people, when talking about free will, talk of things which they do not at all understand. 'Now,' says one, 'I believe men can be saved if they will.' My dear sir, that is not the question at all. The question is, are men ever found naturally willing to submit to the humbling terms of the gospel of Christ? We declare, upon Scriptural authority, that the human will is so desperately set on mischief, so depraved, and so inclined to everything that is evil, and so disinclined to everything that is good, that without the powerful, super-natural, irresistible influence of the Holy Spirit, no human being will ever be constrained toward Christ" (C. H. Spurgeon).

"Now here is a threefold cord against heaven and holiness, not easily to be broken; a blind man, a perverse will, and disorderly, distempered affec-tions. The mind, swelled with self-conceit, says the man should not stoop; the will, opposite to the will of God, says he will not; and the corrupt affections rising against the Lord, in defense of the corrupt will, says he shall not. Thus the poor creature stands out against God and goodness, till a day of power come, in which he is made a new creature" (T. Boston). Perhaps some readers are inclined to say, "Such teaching as this is calcu-lated to discourage sinners and drive them to despair." Our answer is, first, that it is according to God's Word! Second, oh, that it may please Him to use this truth to drive some to despair of all help from themselves. Third, it makes manifest the absolute necessity of the Holy Spirit's working with such depraved and spiritually helpless creatures, if they are ever to come savingly to Christ. And until this is clearly perceived *His* aid will never be *really* sought in earnest!

13 Coming to Christ With Our Understanding

There are some souls greatly distressed and puzzled to know exactly what is signified by "coming to Christ." They have read and heard the words often, and perhaps many a preacher has bidden them to "come to Him," yet without giving a Scriptural explanation of what that term connotes. Such as have been awakened by the Spirit, shown their woeful condition, convicted of their high-handed and life-long rebellion against God, and brought to realize their dire need of Christ, and who are truly anxious to come savingly to Him, have found it a task altogether beyond their powers. Their cry is, "Oh, that I knew where I might find him! that I might come even to his seat!" (Job 23:3). True, there are not many who pass through such an experience, for *God's* "flock" is but a "little" one (Luke 12:32). True, the vast majority of professing Christians claim that *they* found "coming to Christ" a very simple matter. But in the clear light of John 6:44, we must assure you, dear reader, that if *you* found "coming to Christ" to be easy, then it is proof you have *never* come to Him at all in a spiritual and saving way.

What, then, is meant by "coming to Christ"? First, and negatively, let it be pointed out that it is *not* an act which we perform by any of our bodily members. This is so obvious that there should be no need for us to make the statement. But in these awful days of spiritual ignorance and the carnal perversion of the holy things of God, explanation of the most elementary truths and terms is really required. When so many precious souls have been deluded into thinking that a going forward to a "mourner's bench" or "penitent form," or the taking of some preacher's hand, is the same thing as coming to Christ, we dare not pass over the defining of this apparently simple term, nor ignore the need for pointing out what it does not signify.

Second, the word "come," when used in this connection, is a *metaphorical* one: that is to say, a word which expresses an act of the body is transferred to the soul, to denote its act. To "come to Christ" signifies the movement of a Spirit-enlightened mind toward the Lord Jesus—as Prophet, to be instructed by Him; as Priest, whose atonement and intercession are to be relied upon; as King, to be ruled by Him. Coming to Christ implies a turning of our back upon the world, and a turning unto Him as our only Hope and Portion. It is a going out of self so as to rest no longer on anything in self. It is the abandoning of every idol and of all other dependencies, the heart going out to Him in loving submission and trustful confidence. It is the will surrendering to Him as Lord, ready to accept His yoke, take up the cross, and follow Him without reserve.

To "come to Christ" is the turning of the whole soul unto a whole Christ in the exercise of divine grace upon him: it is the mind, heart, and will being supernaturally drawn to Him, so as to trust, love, and serve Him. "It is the duty and interest of weary and heavy-laden sinners to 'come to Christ'—renouncing all those things which stand in opposition to Him, or in competition with Him, we must accept Him as our Physician and Advocate, and give up ourselves to His conduct and government, freely willing to be saved by Him, in His own way, and on His own terms" (Matthew Henry). Ere proceeding farther, we would earnestly beg each reader prayerfully and carefully to test and measure himself or herself by what has been said in this and the preceding paragraph. Take nothing for granted; as you value your soul, seek divine help to make sure that you have *truly* "come to Christ."

Now a popish "christ" is a christ of *wood,* and a false preacher's "christ" is a christ of *words;* but Christ Jesus, our Lord, is "the mighty God, the everlasting Father, the Prince of Peace" (Isaiah 9:6). The Christ of God fills heaven and earth; He is the One by whom all things exist and consist. He is seated at the right hand of the Majesty on high, having all power, dominion, and might. He is made higher than the heavens, and unto Him all principalities and powers are subject. At His presence both the earth and the heavens shall yet flee away. Such a Christ is not to be offered or proffered, sold or given, by sinful men. He is the unspeakable Gift of the Father to as many as He has ordained to eternal life, and none others. This Christ, this Gift of the Father, is supernaturally revealed and applied to the heirs of salvation by the Holy Spirit, when, where, and as He pleases; and not when, where, and how men please.

In the previous chapter we dwelt at length upon the words in John 6:44, "No man can come unto me," seeking to show the nature of the fallen creature's spiritual impotence, or why it is that the unregenerate are unable to come to Christ in a spiritual and saving way. Let us now ponder the remainder of our Lord's sentence: "except the Father which hath sent me draw him." Of what does that "drawing" consist? We answer, first, that just as our "coming to Christ" does not refer to any bodily action, so this divine "drawing" respects not the employment of any external force. Second, it signifies a powerful impulse put forth by the Holy Spirit with the elect, whereby their native impotence for performing spiritual actions is overcome, and an ability for the same is imparted. It is this secret and effectual operation of the Spirit upon the human soul that enables and causes it to come to Christ.

A. *A knowledge of Christ is essential.* There can be no movement toward an unknown object. No one can obey a command until he is acquainted with its terms. A prop must be seen before it will be rested on. We must have some acquaintance with a person before he will either be trusted or loved. This principle is so obvious that it needs arguing no further. Apply it to the case in hand, the subject before us: the knowledge of Christ must of necessity precede our believing on Him or our coming to Him. "How shall they believe in him of whom they have not heard?" (Rom. 10:14), "He that cometh to God *must* believe that he is, and that he is a rewarder of them that diligently seek him" (Heb. 11:6). None can come to Christ while they are ignorant about Him. As it was in the old creation, so it is in the new: God first says, "Let there be light."

B. *This knowledge of Christ comes to the mind from the Holy Scriptures.* Nothing can be known of Him save that which God has been pleased to reveal concerning Him in the Word of Truth. It is there alone that the "true doctrine of Christ" (II John 9) is found. Therefore did our Lord give commandment, "Search the scriptures . . . they are they which testify of me" (John 5:39). When He berated the two disciples for their slowness of heart to believe, we are told that "beginning at Moses and all the prophets, he expounded unto them in all the scriptures the things concerning himself" (Luke 24:27). The Divine Oracles are designated "the word of Christ" (Col. 3:16) because He is the substance of them. Where the Scriptures have not gone, Christ is unknown; clear proof is this that an acquaintance with Him cannot be gained apart from their inspired testimony.

C. *A theoretical knowledge of Christ is not sufficient.* Upon this point we must dilate at greater length, for much ignorance concerning it prevails today. A head knowledge about Christ is very frequently mistaken for a heart acquaintance with Him. But orthodoxy is not salvation. A carnal judgment about Christ, a mere intellectual knowledge of Him, will never bring a dead sinner to His feet: there must be a living experience—God's Word and work meeting together in the soul, renewing the understanding. As I Corinthians 13:2 so plainly and solemnly warns us, I may have the gift of prophecy, understand all mysteries, and all knowledge, yet if I have not love, I am nothing. Just as a blind man may, through labor and diligence, acquire an accurate theoretical or notional conception of many subjects and objects which he never saw, so the natural man may by religious education and personal effort obtain a sound doctrinal knowledge of the person and work of Christ, without having any spiritual or vital acquaintance with Him.

Not every kind of knowledge, even of God's Truth and His Christ, is effectual and saving. There is a *form* of knowledge, as well as of godliness, which is destitute of power—"which hast the form of knowledge and of the truth in the law" (Rom. 2:20). The reference is to the Jews, who were instructed in the Scriptures, and considered themselves well qualified to teach others; yet the Truth had not been written on their hearts by the Holy Spirit. A *"form of knowledge"* signifies that there was a model of it in their brains, so that they were able to discourse freely and fluently upon the things of God, yet were they without the life of God in their souls. Oh, how many have a knowledge of salvation, yet not a knowledge *unto* salvation, as the apostle distinguishes it in II Timothy 3:15—such a knowledge as the latter must be imparted to the soul by the miracle-working operation of the Holy Spirit.

"They proceed from evil to evil, and *they know not me,* saith the Lord" (Jer. 9:3). Of whom was this spoken—of the heathen who were without any written revelation from Him? *No,* of Israel, who had His law in their hands, His temple in their midst, His prophets speaking to them. They had been favored with many and wondrous manifestations of His majesty, holiness, power, and mercy; yet though they had much intellectual knowledge of Him they were strangers to Him spiritually. So it was when the Son of God became incarnate. How much *natural* light they had concerning Him: they witnessed His perfect life, saw His wondrous miracles, heard His matchless teaching, were frequently in His immediate presence; yet, though the light showed in the darkness, "the darkness comprehended it not" (John 1:5). So it is today. Reader, you may be a diligent student of the New Testament, be thoroughly acquainted with the Old Testament types and prophecies, believe all that the Scriptures say concerning Christ, and earnestly teach them to others, and yet be yourself a stranger to Him spiritually.

"Except a man be born again, he cannot *see* the kingdom of God" (John 3:3), which means that the unregenerate are utterly incapable of discerning the things of God spiritually. True, they may "see" them in a natural way: they may investigate and even admire them theoretically, but receive them in an experimental and vital way they cannot. As this distinction is of such great importance, and yet so little known today, let us endeavor to illustrate it. Imagine a man who has never heard any music: others tell him of its beauty and charm, and he decides to make a careful study of it. That man might thoroughly familiarize himself with the art of music, learn all the rules of that art, so that he understood the proportions and harmony of it; but what a different thing is that from listening to a grand oratorio—the ear now taking in what before the mind knew only the theory of! Still greater is the difference between a natural and a spiritual knowledge of divine things.

The apostle declares, "We speak the word of God in a mystery" (I Cor. 2:7). He did not only affirm that it is a mystery in itself, but that it is still spoken "*in* a mystery." And why is this? Because the unregenerate, even where it is spoken in their hearing, yea, when it is clearly apprehended by them in a notional way, neither know nor apprehend the mystery that is still in it. Proverbs 9:10 declares that "the knowledge of the holy is understanding": there is no true understanding of divine things except the "knowledge of the holy." Every real Christian has a knowledge of divine things, a personal, experimental, vital knowledge of them, which no carnal man possesses, or can obtain, no matter how diligently he studies them. If I have seen the picture of a man, I have an image in my mind of that man according to his picture; but if I see the man himself, how different is the image of him which is then formed in my mind! Far greater still is the difference between Christ made known in the Scriptures and Christ "revealed *in me*" (Gal. 1:16).

D. *There must be a spiritual and supernatural knowledge of Christ imparted by the Holy Spirit.* This is in view of I John 5:20, "We know that the Son of God is come, and hath *given us an understanding,* that we may know him that is true." The faculty must be suited to the object or subject known. The natural understanding is capable of taking in Christ and knowing Him in a natural way, but we must be "renewed in the spirit of our mind" (Eph. 4:23) before we can know Christ in a spiritual way. There must be a supernatural work of grace wrought upon the mind by the Holy Spirit before there can be any inward and spiritual apprehension of the supernatural and spiritual person of Christ. That is the true and saving knowledge of Christ which fires the affections, sanctifies the will, and raises up the mind to a spiritual fixation on the Rock of Ages. It is *this* knowledge of Him which is "life eternal" (John 17:3). It is *this* knowledge which produces faith in Christ, love for Him, submission to Him. It is *this* knowledge which causes the soul truthfully and joyously to exclaim, "Whom have I in heaven but thee? and there is none upon earth that I desire beside thee" (Ps. 73:25).

"No man can come to me, except the Father which hath sent me draw him" (John 6:44). It is by the secret and effectual operation of the Spirit that the Father brings each of His elect to a saving knowledge of Christ. These operations of the Spirit begin by His enlightening the understanding, renewing the mind. Observe carefully the order in Ezekiel 37:14, "And shall put my spirit in you, and ye shall live . . . *then* shall ye *know* that I the Lord have spoken it." No sinner ever comes to Christ until the Holy Spirit first comes to him! And no sinner will savingly believe on Christ until the Spirit has communicated faith to him (Eph. 2:8; Col. 2:12); and even then, faith is an eye to *discern* Christ before it is a foot to *approach Him.* There can be no act without an object, and there can be no exercising of faith upon Christ till Christ is seen in His excellency, sufficiency, and suitability to poor sinners. "That he may know *and* believe me" (Isa. 43:10) is the order. "They that *know* thy name will [not "ought to"] put their trust in thee" (Ps. 9:10). But again we say that knowledge must be a spiritual and miraculous one imparted by the Spirit.

The Spirit Himself, and not merely a preacher, must take of the things of Christ and show them unto the heart. It is only in *God's* "light" that we truly "*see*" light" (Ps. 36:9). The opening of his eyes preceded the conversion of the sinner from Satan unto God (Acts 26:18). The light of the sun is seen breaking out at the dawn of day, before its heat is felt. It is those who "see" the Son with a supernaturally enlightened understanding who "believe" on Him with a spiritual and saving faith (John 6:40). We *behold* as in a mirror the glory of the Lord before we are *changed* into *His* very image (II Cor. 3:18). Note the order in Romans 3:11, "there is none that understandeth" goes before "there is none that seeketh after God." The Spirit must shed His light upon the understanding, which light conveys the actual image of spiritual things in a spiritual way to the mind, forming them on the soul; much as a sensitive photographic plate receives the light from the images to which it is exposed. *This* is the "demonstration of the Spirit and of power" (I Cor. 2:4).

E. *How is this spiritual and vital knowledge to be known from a mere theoretical and notional one? By its effects.* To the Thessalonians Paul wrote, "For our gospel came not unto you in *word only,* but *also in power,* and in the Holy Spirit, and in much assurance" (I Thess. 1:5), which is partly explained in the next verse, "having received the word in much affliction, with joy of the Holy Spirit." The Spirit had given that Word in efficacy which no logic, rhetoric, or persuasive power of men could give it. It had smitten the conscience, torn open the wounds which sin had made, exposed its festering sores. It had pierced them even to the dividing asunder of soul and spirit. It had slain their good opinion of themselves. It had made them feel the wrath of God burning against them. It had caused them seriously to question if such wretches could possibly find mercy at the hands of the holy God. It had communicated faith to look upon the great Physician of souls. It had given a joy such as this poor world knows nothing of.

The light which the Spirit imparts to the understanding is full of efficacy, whereas that which men acquire through their study is not so. Ordinary and strong mineral waters are alike in color, but differ much in their taste and virtue. A carnal man may acquire a theoretical knowledge of all that a spiritual man knows vitally, yet is he "barren" and "unfruitful" in the knowledge of our Lord Jesus Christ (II Peter 1:8). The light he has is ineffectual, for it does not purify his heart, renew his will, or transform his life. The head knowledge of divine truth, which is all that multitudes of present-day professing Christians possess, has no more influence upon their walk unto practical godliness than though it was stored up in some other man's brains. The light which the Spirit gives humbles and abases its recipient; the knowledge which is acquired by education and personal efforts puffs up and fills the carnal deceit.

A spiritual and saving knowledge of Christ always constrains the soul unto loving obedience. No sooner did the light of Christ shine into Paul's heart than he at once asked, "Lord, what wilt thou have me do?" (Acts 9:6). Of the Colossians the apostle declared, "The gospel which is come unto you . . . bringeth forth fruit . . . since the day ye heard of it, and knew the grace of God in truth" or "in reality" (1:5-6). But a mere intellectual knowledge of the truth is "held in *unrighteousness*" (Rom. 1:18). Its possessors are zealous to argue and cavil about it, and look down with contempt upon all who are not as wise as they; yet the *lives* of these frequently put them to shame. A saving knowledge of Christ so endears Him to the soul that all else is esteemed as dung in comparison with His excellency: the light of His glory has cast a complete eclipse over all that is in the world. But a mere doctrinal knowledge of Christ produces no such effects: while its possessors may loudly sing His praises, their hearts are still coveting and eagerly pursuing the things of time and sense.

The natural man may know the truth of the things of God, but not the things themselves. He may thoroughly understand the Scriptures in the letter of them, but not in their spirit. He may discourse of them in a sound and orthodox manner, but in no other way than one can *talk* of honey and vinegar who never tasted the sweetness of the one or the sourness of the other. There are hundreds of preachers who have accurate notions of spiritual things, but who see and taste not the things themselves which are wrapped in the words of Truth, "understanding neither what they say, nor whereof they affirm" (I Tim. 1:7). Just as an astronomer who makes a life study of the stars knows their names, their positions, and varying magnitudes, yet receives no more personal and special influence from them than do other men, so it is with those who study the Scriptures but are not supernaturally and savingly enlightened by the Spirit. Oh, my reader, has the Day Star arisen *in your heart* (II Peter 1:19)?

The distinction pointed out between a sound intellectual knowledge of Christ and a vital and transforming knowledge of Him, between knowing Christ as He is set forth in the Scriptures and as He is divinely revealed in us (Gal. 1:16), is not one which will appeal to the carnal mind; rather is it one which will be contemptuously rejected.

But what has been said *does not* clash, in the slightest degree, with I Corinthians 2:14, when that verse is rightly read and understood. Let it be carefully noted that it does not say the *"things of God* are foolishness" unto the natural man. Had it done so, the writer had been at a complete loss to explain it. No, it declares that the *"things of the Spirit* of God" are foolishness; and what has been said only serves to illustrate the minute accuracy of this verse. The "things of God" these men profess to believe; the "things of Christ" they appear valiantly to champion; but the "things of *the Spirit of God"* they are personal strangers unto; and, therefore, when His secret and mysterious work upon the souls of God's elect is pressed upon them they appear to be so much "foolishness" unto them — either "mysticism" or "fanaticism." But to the renewed it is far otherwise.

The Spirit's supernatural operations in the implanting of faith in God's elect (Col. 2:12) produce a "new creation." Salvation by faith is wrought through the Spirit's working effectually with the gospel. Then it is that He *forms* Christ in the soul (Gal. 4:19), and lets in the Object of faith through the eye of faith, a real "image" of Christ being directly stamped upon the newly quickened soul, which quickening has given ability to discern Christ. Thus Christ is "formed" in the heart, after the manner that an outward object is formed in the eye. When I say that I have a certain man or object in my eye, I do not mean that this man or object is in my eye *locally* — that is impossible. But they are in my eye *objectively* — I *see* them. So when it is said that Christ is *"formed* in us," that Christ is *"in* us the hope of glory" (Col. 1:27), it is not to be understood that He who is now corpore-ally at the right hand of God is *locally and substantially* formed in us. No, but that Christ at the right hand of God, the substance and *object* of faith, is by the Spirit let in from above, so that the soul sees Him by the eye of faith, exactly as He is represented in the Word. *So* Christ is "formed" in us; and thus He "dwells in our hearts by faith" (Eph. 3:17).

What we have endeavored to set forth above is beautifully adumbrated in the lower and visible world. It is indeed striking to discover how much of God's spiritual works are shadowed out in the material realm. If our minds were but more spiritual, and our eyes engaged in a keener lookout, we should find signs and symbols on every side of the invisible realities of God. On a sunshiny day, when a man looks into clear water, he sees there a face (his own), formed by representation, which directly answers to the face outside and above the water; there are not two faces, but one, original and yet represented. But only one face is seen, casting its own single image upon the water. So it is in the soul's history of God's elect: "But we all, with open face beholding as in a glass the glory of the Lord, *are changed into the same image* from glory to glory, even *as by the Spirit of* the Lord" (II Cor. 3:18). Oh, that His image in us may be more evident to others.

14 Coming to Christ With Our Affections

All that the Father giveth me shall come unto me" (John 6:37), declares the Lord Jesus. He, who before the foundation of the world gave the *persons* of His people unto Christ, now gives them, in regeneration, a *heart* for Christ. The "heart" includes the affections as well as the understanding. In our last chapter we pointed out how that no man will (or can) "come to Christ" while ignorant of Him. It is equally true that no man will (or can) "come to Christ" while his affections are alienated from Him. Not only is the understanding of the natural man shrouded in total darkness, but his heart is thoroughly opposed to God. "The carnal mind is enmity [not merely "at enmity," but "enmity itself"] against God" (Rom. 8:7); and "enmity" is something more than a train of hostile thoughts, it is the hatred of the affections themselves. Therefore, when the Holy Spirit makes a man a "new creature in Christ" He not only renews his understanding, but He radically changes the heart.

When faith gives us a sight of spiritual things, the heart is warmed with love to them. Note the order in Hebrews 11:13, where, in connection with the patriarchs' faith in God's promises, we are told, "were persuaded of them, and *embraced* them," which is a term denoting great affection. When the understanding is renewed by the Spirit, then the heart is drawn unto Christ, with a tender desire for Him. When the Holy Spirit is pleased to make known in the soul the wondrous love of Christ to me, then love unto Him is begotten and goes out toward Him in return. Observe the order in I John 4:16, "And we have known and believed the love that God hath to us. God is love; and he that dwelleth in love dwelleth in God, and God in him": the apostle places knowledge (not intellectual, but spiritual) before faith, and both before a union and communion with divine love. The light and knowledge of Christ and heaven which we have by tradition, education, hearing, or reading never fires the affections. But when the love of God is "shed abroad in our hearts by the Holy Spirit" (Rom. 5:5) what a difference is produced!

Far too little emphasis has been placed upon this aspect of our subject. In proof of this assertion, weigh carefully the following question: Why is it that "he that *believeth not* shall be damned" (Mark 16:16) is quoted a hundred times more frequently by preachers and tract writers than "if any man *love* not the Lord Jesus, let him be accursed" (I Cor. 16:22)? If we are properly to preserve the balance of truth, we must note carefully the manner in which the Holy Spirit has rung the changes on "believe" and "love" in the New Testament. Consider the following passages: "All things work together for good to them that [not trust, but] *love* God" (Rom. 8:28); "Them that [not only believe, but] *love* him" (I Cor. 2:9): "If any man *love* God, the same is known [or approved] of him" (I Cor. 8:3): "A crown of righteousness which the Lord, the righteous judge, shall give me in that day: and not to me only, but unto all them that [not believe in, but] *love* his appearing" (II Tim. 4:8); "The crown of life, which the Lord hath promised to them that *love* him" (James 1:12); "Heirs of the kingdom which he hath promised to them that love him" (James 2:5); "He that *loveth not* knoweth not God; for God is love" (I John 4:8).

"No man can come to me, except the Father which hath sent me draw him" (John 6:44). In our last chapter we saw that this "drawing" consists, in part, of the Spirit's supernatural enlightenment of the understanding. It also consists in the Spirit's inclining the affections toward Christ. He acts upon sinners agreeably to their nature; not by external force, such as is used on an unwilling animal, but by spiritual influence or power moving their inward faculties: "I drew them with cords of a *man,* with bands of *love*" (Hos. 11:4)—by rational conviction of their judgment, by showing them that there is infinitely more goodness and blessedness in Christ than in the creature or the sinful gratification of carnal desires; by winning their hearts to Christ, by communicating to them a powerful sense of His superlative excellency and complete suitability unto all their needs. To them that believe "he is *precious*" (I Peter 2:7)—so precious that they are willing to part with the world and everything else in order that they may "win Christ" (Phil. 3:8).

As was shown at some length in the opening chapter, the affections of the natural man are alienated from God, wedded to the things of time and sense, so that he will not come to Christ. Though God's servants seek to charm him with the lovely music of the gospel, like the adder he closes his ear. It is as the Lord portrayed it in the parable of the great supper: "They all with one consent began to make excuse" (Luke 14:18), one preferring his lands, another his merchandise, another his social recreation. And nothing short of the almighty power and working of the Holy Spirit in the heart can break the spell which sin and Satan have cast over man, and turn his heart from perishing objects to an imperishable one. This He does in God's elect by His secret and invincible operations, sweetly working in and alluring them by revealing Christ to them in the winsomeness of His person, and the infinite riches of His grace, by letting down His love into their hearts, and by moving them to lay hold of His kind invitations and precious promises.

Most blessedly is this represented to us in "*my* beloved put in his hand by the hole of the door, and my bowels were moved for him" (Song of Sol. 5:4). Here the door of the heart (Acts 14:14), or, more specifically, the "door of faith" (Acts 14:27), is seen shut against Christ, and the object of His love loath and unwilling to rise and open to Him. But, though unwelcome, His love cannot be quenched, and He gently enters (He does not burst the door open!) uninvited. His "hand" opening the "door" is a figure of His efficacious grace removing every obstacle in the heart of His elect (cf. Acts 11:21), and winning it to Himself. The effect of His gracious entry, by His Spirit, is seen in the "and my bowels were moved for him," which is a figure of the stirring of the affections after Him (cf. Isa. 63:15; Philem. 12). (For the thoughts of this paragraph we are indebted to the incomparable commentary of John Gill on the Song of Solomon.)

What a miracle of grace has been wrought when the heart is truly turned from the world unto God, from self unto Christ, from love of sin unto love of holiness! It is this which is the fulfilment of God's covenant promise in Ezekiel 34:26, "A new heart also will I give you, and a new spirit will I put within you; and I will take away the stony heart out of your flesh, and I will give you an heart of flesh." There is no man who loves money so much, but that he is willing to part with it for that which he values more highly than the sum he parts with to purchase it. The natural man esteems material things more highly than he does spiritual, but the regenerated loves Christ more than all other objects besides, and this because he has been made a "new creature." It is a spiritual love which binds the heart to Christ.

It is not simply a knowledge of the Truth which saves, but a *love* of it which is the essential prerequisite. This is clear from II Thessalonians 2:10, "Because they received not the love of the truth, that they might be saved." Close attention must be paid unto those words, or a wrong conclusion may be drawn; it is not a love *for* the Truth, but a love *of* the Truth. There are those who have the former, but are destitute of the latter. We have met Russellites, and have boarded with Christadelphians, who put many a real Christian to shame; people who after a long day's work spent the whole evening in diligently studying the Bible. Nor was it to satisfy curiosity. Their zeal had lasted for years. Their Bible was as precious to them as "beads" or "rosary" are to a devout Romanist. So, too, there is a *natural* "love" for Christ, an ardent devotion for Him, which springs not from a renewed heart. Just as one reared among devout Romanists grows up with a deep veneration and genuine affection for the virgin, so one carefully trained by Protestant parents, told from infancy that Jesus loves him, grows up with a real but natural love for Him.

There may be a historical faith in all the doctrines of Scripture where the power of them is never experienced. There may be a fleshly zeal for portions of God's Truth (as there was in the case of the Pharisees) and yet the heart not be renewed. There may be joyous emotions felt by a superficial reception of the Word (as there was in the stony-ground hearers—Matt. 13:20) where the "root of the matter" (Job. 19:28) be lacking. Tears may flow freely at the pathetic sight of the suffering Saviour (as with the company of women who bewailed Christ as He journeyed to the cross—Luke 23:27-28), and yet the heart be as hard as the nether millstone toward God. There may be a rejoicing in the light of God's Truth (as was the case with Herod—Mark 6:20), and yet hell never be escaped from.

Since, then, there is a love *for* the Truth in contradistinction from a love *of* the Truth, and a natural love for Christ in contrast with a spiritual love of Him, how am I to be sure which mine is? We may distinguish between these "loves" thus: First, the one is partial, the other is impartial; the one esteems the doctrines of Scripture but not the duties it enjoins, the promises of Scripture but not the precepts, the blessings of Christ but not His claims, His priestly office but not His kingly rule; but not so with the spiritual lover. Second, the one is occasional, the other is regular; the former balks when personal interests are crossed, not so the latter. Third, the one is evanescent and weak, the other lasting and powerful; the former quickly wanes when other delights compete, and prevails not to control the other affections; the latter rules the heart, and is strong as death. Fourth, the former betters not its possessor; the latter transforms the life.

That a saving "coming to Christ" *is* the affections being turned to and fixed upon Him may be further demonstrated from the nature of backsliding, which begins with the heart's departure from Christ. Observe how this is traced to its real source in Revelation 2:4, "Thou hast left [not lost] thy first *love.*" The reality and genuineness of our *returning* to Christ are evidenced by the *effects* which the workings of the understanding produce upon the affections. A striking example of this is found in Matthew 26:75, "And Peter remembered the word of Jesus, which said unto him, Before the cock crow, thou shalt deny me thrice. And he went out, and wept bitterly"; that "remembrance" was not merely a historical one, but a gracious one—his heart was melted by it. So it ever is when the Holy Spirit works in and "renews" us. I may recall a past sin without being duly humbled thereby. I may "remember" Christ's death in a mechanical and speculative way, without the affections being truly moved. It is only as the faculty of our understanding is quickened by the Holy Spirit that the heart is powerfully impressed.

15 Coming to Christ With Our Will

The man within the body is possessed of three principal faculties: the understanding, the affections, and the will. As was shown in the first chapter, all of these were radically affected by the Fall: they were defiled and corrupted, and in consequence they are used in the service of self and sin rather than of God and of Christ. But in regeneration these faculties are quickened and cleansed by the Spirit: not completely, but initially and continuously so in the lifelong process of sanctification, and perfectly so at our glorification. Now each of these three faculties is subordinated to the others by the order of nature, that is as man had been constituted by his Maker. In Genesis 3:6, we read, "The woman saw [perceived] that the tree was good for food [that was a conclusion drawn by the understanding], and that it was *pleasant* to the eyes [there was response of her affections], and a tree to be desired [there was the moving of the will] . . . she took [there was the completed action]."

Now the motions of divine grace work through the apprehensions of faith in the understanding, these warming and firing the affections, and they in turn influencing and moving the will. Every faculty of the soul is put forth in a saving "coming to Christ": "If thou believest with *all* thine heart, thou mayest"—be baptized (Acts 8:37). "Coming to Christ" is more immediately an act of the will, as John 5:40 shows; yet the will is not active toward Him until the understanding has been enlightened and the affections quickened. The Spirit first causes the sinner to perceive his deep need of Christ, and this by showing him his fearful rebellion against God, and that none but Christ can atone for the same. Secondly, the Spirit creates in the heart a desire after Christ, and this by making him sick of sin and in love with holiness. Third, as the awakened and enlightened soul has been given to see the glory and excellency of Christ, and His perfect suitability to the lost and perishing sinner, then the Spirit draws out the will to set the highest value on that excellency, to esteem it far above all else, and to close with Him.

As there is a divine order among the three Persons of the Godhead in providing salvation, so there is in the applying or bestowing of it. It was God the Father's good pleasure in appointing His people from eternity unto salvation that was the most full and sufficient *impulsive* cause of their salvation, and every whit able to produce its effect. It was the incarnate Son of God whose obedience and sufferings were the most complete and sufficient *meritorious* cause of their salvation, to which nothing can be added to make it more apt and able to secure the travail of His soul. Yet neither the one nor the other can *actually* save any sinner except as the Spirit *applies* Christ to it: His work becomes the *efficient* and immediate cause of their salvation. In like manner, the sinner is not saved when his understanding is enlightened and his affections fired: there must also be the act of the will, surrendering to God and laying hold of Christ.

The order of the Spirit's operations corresponds to the three great offices of Christ the Mediator, namely His prophetic, priestly, and kingly. As Prophet, He is first apprehended by the understanding, the Truth of God being received from His lips. As Priest, He is trusted and loved by the heart or affections, His glorious person being first endeared unto the soul by the gracious work which He performed for it. As Potentate, our will must be subdued unto Him, so that we submit to His government, yield to His scepter, and heed His commandments. Nothing short of the throne of our hearts will satisfy the Lord Jesus.

"No man can come to me, except the Father which hath sent me draw him" (John 6:44). This "drawing" is accomplished by the Spirit: first, in effectually enlightening the understanding; second, by quickening the affections; third, by freeing the will from the bondage of sin and inclining it toward God. By the invincible workings of grace the Spirit turns the bent of that will, which before moved only toward sin and vanity, unto Christ. "Thy people," said God unto the Mediator, "shall be willing in the day of thy power" (Ps. 110:3). Yet though divine power be put forth upon a human object, the Spirit does not infringe the will's prerogative of acting freely; He morally persuades it. He subdues it. He subdues its sinful intractability. He overcomes its prejudice, wins and draws it by the sweet attractions of grace.

The perfect consistency between the freedom of a regenerated man's spiritual actions and the efficacious grace of God moving him thereto is seen in II Corinthians 8:16-17. "But thanks be to God, which put the same earnest care into the heart of Titus for you. For indeed he accepted the exhortation; but being more forward, of his own accord he went unto you." Titus was moved to that work by Paul's exhortation, and was willing of his own accord to engage therein; and yet it was "God which put the same earnest care into the heart of Titus" for them. God controls the inward feelings and acts of men without interfering with either their liberty or responsibility. The zeal of Titus was the spontaneous effusion of his own heart, and was an index to and element of his character; nevertheless, God wrought in him both to will and to do of *His* good pleasure.

No sinner savingly "comes to Christ," or truly receives Him into the heart, until the will freely consents (not merely "assents" in a theoretical way) to the severe and self-denying terms upon which He is presented in the gospel. No sinner is prepared to forsake all for Christ, take up "the cross" and "follow" Him in the path of universal obedience, until the heart genuinely esteems Him "the fairest among ten thousand," and this none ever to do before the understanding has been supernaturally enlightened and the affections supernaturally quickened. Obviously, none will espouse themselves with conjugal affections to that person whom they account not the best that can be chosen. It is as the Spirit convicts us of our emptiness and shows us Christ's fullness, our guilt and His righteousness, our filthiness and the cleansing merits of His blood, our depravity and His holiness, that the heart is won and the resistance of the will is overcome.

The holy and spiritual Truth of God finds nothing akin to itself in the unregenerate soul, but instead everything that is opposed to it (John 15:18; Rom. 8:7). The demands of Christ are too humbling to our natural pride, too searching for the callous conscience, too exacting for our fleshly desires. And a miracle of grace has to be wrought within us before this awful depravity of our nature, this dreadful state of affairs, is changed. That miracle of grace consists in overcoming the resistance which is made by indwelling sin, and creating desires and longing Christward; and then it is that the will cries,

> Nay, but I yield, I yield,
> I can hold out no more;
> I sink, by dying love compell'd,
> And own Thee Conqueror.

A beautiful illustration of this is found in Ruth 1:14-18. Naomi, a backslidden saint, is on the point of leaving the far country, and (typically) returning to her Father's house. Her two daughters-in-law wish to accompany her. Faithfully did Naomi bid them "count the cost" (Luke 14:28); instead of at once urging them to act on their first impulse, she pointed out the difficulties and trials to be encountered. This was too much for Orpah: her "goodness" (like that of the stony-ground hearers, and myriads of others) was only "as a morning cloud," and "as the early dew" it quickly went away (Hos. 6:4). In blessed contrast with this we read that Ruth "clave unto her," saying, "Intreat me not to leave thee, or

to return from following after thee: for whither thou goest I will go; and
where thou lodgest I will lodge: thy people shall be my people, and thy
God my God."

What depth and loveliness of affection were here! What wholehearted
self-surrender! See Ruth freely and readily leaving her own country and
kindred, tearing herself from every association of nature, turning a deaf ear
to her mother-in-law's begging her to return to her gods (v. 15) and people.
See her renouncing idolatry and all that flesh holds dear, to be a worshiper
and servant of the living God, counting all things but loss for the sake of
His favor and salvation; and her future conduct proved her faith was
genuine and her profession sincere. Ah, naught but a miraculous work of
God in her soul can explain this. It was God working in her "both to will
and to do of *His* good pleasure" (Phil. 2:13).

The relation between our understanding being enlightened and the affections quickened by God, and the resultant consent of the will, is seen in
Psalm 119:34: "Give me understanding, and I shall keep thy law; yea, I
shall observe it with my whole heart." "The sure result of regeneration, or
the bestowal of understanding, is the devout reverence for the law and a
reverent keeping of it in the heart. The Spirit of God makes us to know
the Lord and to understand somewhat of His love, wisdom, holiness, and
majesty; and the result is that we honor the law and yield our hearts to the
obedience of the faith. The understanding operates upon the affections; it
convinces the heart of the beauty of the law, so that the soul loves it with
all its powers; and then it reveals the majesty of the Lawgiver, and the
whole nature bows before His supreme will. He alone obeys God who can
say, 'My Lord, I would serve Thee, and do it with all my heart': and none
can truly say this till they have received as a free grant the inward illumination of the Holy Spirit" (C. H. Spurgeon).

Ere turning to our final section, a few words need to be added here on
I Peter 2:4, "To whom coming, as unto a living stone . . . ye also, as lively
stones, are built up a spiritual house." Has the sovereign grace of God
inclined me to come unto Christ? Then it is my duty and interest to
"abide" in Him (John 15:4)—abide in Him by a life of faith daily (Gal.
2:20). It is in this way of continual coming to Christ that we are "built up
a spiritual house." It is in this way that the life of grace is maintained,
until it issues in the life of glory. Faith is to be always receiving out of His
fullness "grace for grace" (John 1:16). Daily should there be the renewed
dedication of myself unto Him and the heart's occupation with Him.

16 Tests to Validate Our Coming to Christ

Unto those who never savingly "came to Christ" He will yet say, "Depart from me, ye cursed, into everlasting fire, prepared for the devil and his angels." The contemplation of those awful words ought almost to freeze the very blood in our veins, searching our consciences and awing our hearts. But, alas, it is much to be feared that Satan will blunt their piercing force to many of our readers, by assuring them that *they have already* come to Christ, and telling them they are fools to doubt it for a moment. But, dear friend, seeing that there is no less than your immortal soul at stake, that whether you spend eternity in heaven with the blessed or in hell with the cursed hinges on whether or not you really and truly "come to Christ," will you not read the paragraphs which follow with double care?

A. *How many rest on their sound doctrinal views of Christ.* They believe firmly in His deity, His holy humanity, His perfect life, His vicarious death, His bodily resurrection, His ascension to God's right hand, His present intercession on high, and His second advent. So, too, did many of those to whom James addressed his Epistle, but he reminded them that "the devils also believe and tremble" (2:19). Oh, my reader, saving faith in Christ is very much more than assenting to the teaching of Scripture concerning Him; it is the giving up of the soul unto Him to be saved, to renounce all else, to yield fully unto Him.

B. *How many mistake the absence of doubts for a proof that they have savingly come to Christ.* They take for granted that for which they have no clear evidence. But, reader, a man possesses not Christ by faith as he does money in a strongbox or title deeds of land which are preserved by his lawyer, and which he never looks at once in a year. No, Christ is as "bread" which a man feeds upon, chews, digests, which his stomach works upon continually, and by which he is nourished and strengthened (John

100

6:53). The empty professor feeds upon a good opinion of himself rather than upon Christ.

C. *How many mistake the stirring of the emotions for the Spirit's quickening of the affections.* If people weep under the preaching of the word, superficial observers are greatly encouraged; and if they go forward to the "mourners' bench" and sob and wail over their sins, this is regarded as a sure sign that God has savingly convicted them. But a supernatural work of divine grace goes much deeper than that. Tears are but on the surface, and are a matter of temperamental constitution—even in nature some of those who feel things the most give the least outward sign of it. It is the weeping of the heart which God requires; it is a godly sorrow for sin, which breaks its reigning power over the soul, that evidences regeneration.

D. *How many mistake a fear of the wrath to come for a hatred of sin.* No one wants to go to hell. If the intellect be convinced of its reality, and the unspeakable awfulness of its torments are in a measure believed, then there may be great uneasiness of mind, fear of conscience, and anguish of heart over the prospect of suffering its eternal burnings. Those fears may last a considerable time, yea, their effects may never completely wear off. The subject of them may come under the ministry of a faithful servant of God, hear him describe the deep ploughing of the Spirit's work, and conclude that he has been the subject of them, yet have none of that love for Christ which manifests itself in a life all the details of which seek to honor and glorify Him.

E. *How many mistake a false peace for a true one.* Let a person who has had awakened within him a natural dread of the lake of fire, whose own conscience has made him wretched, and the preaching he has heard terrified him yet more, then is he not (like a drowning man) ready to clutch at a straw? Let one of the false prophets of the day tell him that all he has to do is to believe John 3:16, and salvation is his, and how eagerly will he—though unchanged in heart—drink in such "smooth things." Assured that nothing more is required than firmly to believe that God loves him and that Christ died for him and his burden is gone, peace now fills him. Yes, and nineteen times out of twenty that "peace" is nothing but Satan's opiate, drugging his conscience and chloroforming him into hell. "There is no [true, spiritual] peace, saith my God, to the wicked," and unless the heart has been purified no man will see God (Matt. 5:8).

F. *How many mistake self-confidence for spiritual assurance.* It is natural for each of us to think well and hope well of ourselves, and to imagine with Haman, "I am the man whom the king delighteth to honour." Perhaps the reader is ready to say, "That is certainly not true of me: so far from having a high esteem, I regard myself as a worthless, sinful creature." Yes, and so deceitful is the human heart, and so ready is Satan to turn everything to his own advantage, that these very lowly thoughts of self may be feasted on and rested on to assure the heart that all is well with you. The apostate King Saul began by having a lowly estimate of himself (I Sam. 9:21).

G. *How many make a promise the sole ground of their faith, and look no farther than the letter of it.* Thus the Jews were deceived by the letter of the law, for they never saw the spiritual meaning of Moses' ministry. In like manner, multitudes are deceived by the letter of such promises as Acts 16:31; Romans 10:13; etc., and look not to Christ in them: they see that He is the jewel in the casket, but rest upon the superscription without, and never lay hold of the Treasure within. But unless the *Person* of Christ be apprehended, unless there be a real surrendering to His lordship, unless He be Himself received into the heart, then believing the letter of the promises will avail nothing.

The above paragraphs have been written in the hope that God may be pleased to arouse some empty professors out of their false security. But lest any of Christ's little ones be stumbled we close with an excerpt from John Bunyan's *Come and Welcome to Jesus Christ:* "How shall we know that such men are coming to Christ? Answer: do they cry out at sin, being burdened with it, as an exceedingly bitter thing? Do they fly from it, as from the face of a deadly serpent? Do they cry out of the insufficiency of their own righteousness, as to justification in the sight of God? Do they cry out after the Lord Jesus to save them? Do they see more worth and merit in one drop of Christ's blood to save them, than in all the sins of the world to damn them? Are they tender of sinning against Jesus Christ? Do they favour Christ in this world, and do they leave all the world for His sake? And are they willing (God helping them) to run hazards for His name, for the love they bear to Him? Are His saints precious to them? If these things be so, these men *are* coming to Christ."

PART FOUR
A Fourfold Salvation

17 Introduction

About 1918 we wrote a booklet entitled *A Threefold Salvation*. It was based on the instruction we had received during our spiritual infancy. Like most of that early teaching, it was defective, because inadequate. As we have continued our study of God's Word, further light has been granted us on this subject—yet, alas, how ignorant we still are—and this has enabled us to see that, in the past, we had started at the wrong point, for instead of beginning at the beginning, we commenced almost in the middle. Instead of salvation from sin being threefold, as we once supposed, we now perceive it to be fourfold. How good is the Lord in vouchsafing us additional light, yet it is now our duty to walk therein, and, as Providence affords us opportunity, to give it out. May the Holy Spirit so graciously guide us that God may be glorified and His people edified.

The subject of God's "so-great-salvation" (Heb. 2:3), as it is revealed to us in the Scriptures and made known in Christian experience, is worthy of a life's study. Anyone who supposes that there is now no longer any need for him to prayerfully search for a fuller understanding of the same, needs to ponder, "If any man think that he knoweth anything, he knoweth nothing yet as he ought to know" (I Cor. 8:2). The fact is that the moment any of us really takes it for granted that he already knows all that there is to be known on *any* subject treated of in Holy Writ, he at once cuts himself off from any further light thereon. That which is most needed by all of us in order to a better understanding of divine things, is not a brilliant intellect, but a truly humble heart and a teachable spirit, and for that we should daily and fervently pray, for we possess it not by nature.

The subject of divine salvation has, sad to say, provoked age-long controversy and bitter contentions even among professing Christians. There is comparatively little real agreement even upon this elementary yet vital truth. Some have insisted that salvation is by divine grace, others have argued it is by human endeavor. A number have sought to defend the middle position, and while allowing that the salvation of a lost sinner must be by divine grace, were not willing to concede that it is by grace *alone*, alleging that God's grace must be plussed by something from the creature, and very varied have been the opinions of what that "something" must be—baptism, church-membership, the performing of good works, holding out faithful to the end, etc. On the other hand, there are those who not only grant that salvation is by grace alone, but who *deny* that God uses any *means* whatever in the accomplishment of His eternal purpose to save His elect—overlooking the fact that the sacrifice of Christ is the grand "means!"

It is true that the church of God was blessed with super-creation blessings, being chosen in Christ before the foundation of the world and predestinated unto the adoption of children, and nothing could or can alter that grand fact. It is equally true that if sin had never entered the world, none had been in need of salvation from it. But sin *has* entered, and the church fell in Adam and came under the curse and condemnation of God's law. Consequently, the elect, equally with the reprobate, shared in the capital offense of their federal head, and partake of its fearful entail: "In Adam all die" (I Cor. 15:22), "By the offence of one judgment came upon *all* men to condemnation" (Rom. 5:18). The result of this is that all are "alienated from the life of God through the ignorance that is in them because of the blindness of their hearts" (Eph. 4:18), so that the members of the mystical Body of Christ are "by nature the children of wrath, even as others" (Eph. 2:3), and hence they are alike in dire need of God's salvation.

Even where there is fundamental soundness in their views upon divine salvation, yet many have such inadequate and one-sided conceptions that other aspects of this truth, equally important and essential, are often overlooked and tacitly denied. How many, for example, would be capable of giving a simple exposition of the following texts: "Who *hath* saved us" (II Tim. 1:9), "*Work out* your own salvation with fear and trembling" (Phil. 2:12), "Now is our salvation *nearer* than when we believed" (Rom. 13:11). Now those verses do not refer to three different salvations, but to three separate aspects of one and unless we learn to distinguish sharply between them, there can be naught but confusion and cloudiness in our thinking. Those passages present three distinct phases and stages of salvation: salvation as an accomplished fact, as a present process, and as a future prospect.

So many today ignore these distinctions, jumbling them together. Some contend for one and argue against the other two; and vice versa. Some insist they are already saved, and deny that they are now being saved. Some declare that salvation is entirely future, and deny that it is in any sense already accomplished. Both are wrong. The fact is that the great majority of professing Christians fail to see that "salvation" is one of the most comprehensive terms in all the Scriptures, including predestination, regeneration, justification, sanctification, and glorification. They have far too cramped an idea of the meaning and scope of the word "salvation" (as it is used in the Scriptures), narrowing its range too much, generally confining their thoughts to but a single phase. They suppose "salvation" means no more than the new birth or the forgiveness of sins. Were one to tell them that salvation is a protracted process, they would view him with suspicion; and if he affirmed that salvation is something awaiting us in the future, they would at once dub him a heretic. Yet *they* would be the ones to err.

Ask the average Christian, "Are you saved?" and he answers, "Yes, I was saved in such and such a year"; and that is as far as his thoughts on the subject go. Ask him, "To what do you owe your salvation?" and "The finished work of Christ" is the sum of his reply. Tell him that each of those answers is seriously defective, and he strongly resents your aspersion. As an example of the confusion which now prevails, we quote the following from a tract on Philippians 2:12, "To whom are those instructions addressed? The opening words of the Epistle tell us: 'To the saints in Christ Jesus'. . . . Thus they were all believers! and could not be required to work for their salvation, for they already possessed it." Alas that so very few today perceive anything wrong in such a statement. Another "Bible teacher" tells us that "save thyself" (I Tim. 4:16) must refer to deliverance from *physical* ills, as Timothy was already saved spiritually. True, yet it is equally true that he was then in process of being saved, and also a fact that his salvation was then future.

Let us now supplement the first three verses quoted and show there are other passages in the New Testament which definitely refer to each distinct *tense* of salvation. First, salvation as *an accomplished fact:* "Thy faith hath saved thee" (Luke 7:50), "by grace ye have been saved" (Greek, and so translated in the Revised Version—Eph. 2:8), "according to His mercy He saved us" (Titus 3:5). Second, salvation as *a present process,* in course of accomplishment, not yet completed: "Unto us which are being saved" (I Cor. 1:18—R.V. and Bag. Interlinear); "Them that believe to the saving [not "salvation"] of the soul" (Heb. 10:39). Third, salvation as *a future prospect:* " . . . sent forth to minister for them who *shall be* heirs of salvation" (Heb. 1:14); "Receive with meekness the engrafted Word, which is able *to save* your souls" (James 1:21); " . . . kept by the power of God through faith *unto* salvation, ready to be revealed in the last time" (I Peter 1:5). Thus, by putting together these different passages we are clearly warranted in formulating the following statement: every genuine Christian has been saved, is now being saved, and will yet be saved—how and from what, we shall endeavor to show.

As further proof of how many-sided is the subject of God's great salvation, and how that in Scripture it is viewed from various angles, take the following: "by *grace* are ye saved" (Eph. 2:8); "saved by His [Christ's] *life*" (i.e.) by His resurrection life (Rom. 5:9); "thy *faith* hath saved thee" (Luke 7:50); "the engrafted *Word* which is able to save your souls" (James 1:21); "saved by *hope*" (Rom. 8:24); "saved yet as by *fire*" (I Cor. 3:15); "the like figure whereunto *baptism* doth also now save us" (I Peter 3:21). Ah, my reader, the Bible is not the lazy man's book, nor can it be soundly expounded by those who do not devote the whole of their time, and that for years, to its prayerful study. It is not that God would bewilder us, but that He would *humble* us, drive us to our knees, make us dependent upon His Spirit. Not to the proud—those who are wise in their own esteem—are its heavenly secrets opened.

In like manner it may be shown from Scripture that the *cause* of salvation is not a single one, as so many suppose—the blood of Christ. Here, too, it is necessary to distinguish between things which differ. First, the *originating* cause of salvation is the eternal purpose of God; or, in other words, the predestinating grace of the Father. Second, the *meritorious* cause of salvation is the mediation of Christ, this having particular respect to the legal side of things; or, in other words, His fully meeting the demands of the law on the behalf and in the stead of those He redeems. Third, the *efficient* cause of salvation is the regenerating and sanctifying operations of the Holy Spirit, which respect the experimental side of it; or, in other words, the Spirit works *in* us what Christ purchased *for* us. Thus, we owe our personal salvation equally to each Person in the Trinity, and not to one (the Son) more than to the others. Fourth, the *instrumental* cause is our faith, obedience, and perseverance: though we are not saved because of them, equally true is it that we cannot be saved (according to God's appointment) without them.

In the opening paragraph we have stated that in our earlier effort we erred as to the starting point. In writing upon a threefold salvation we began with salvation from the penalty of sin, which is our justification. But our salvation does not begin there, as we knew well enough even then; alas that we so blindly followed our erring preceptors. Our salvation originates, of course, in the eternal purpose of God, in His predestinating of us to everlasting glory. "Who hath saved us, and called us with a holy calling, not according to our works, but according to his own purpose and grace, which was given us in Christ Jesus before the world began" (II Tim. 1:9). That has reference to God's *decree* of election: His chosen people were then saved, completely, in the divine purpose, and all that we shall now say has to do with the performing of that purpose, the accomplishing of that decree, the actualization of that salvation.

18 Salvation From the Pleasure of Sin

It is here that God begins in His actual application of salvation unto His elect. God saves us from the pleasure or love of sin before He delivers from the penalty or punishment of sin. Necessarily so, for it would be neither an act of holiness nor of righteousness were He to grant a full pardon to one who was still a rebel against Him, loving that which He hates. God is a God of order throughout, and nothing ever more evidences the perfection of His works than the orderliness of them. And *how* does God save His people from the pleasure of sin? The answer is, "By imparting to them a nature which hates evil and loves holiness." This takes place when they are born again, so that actual salvation begins with regeneration. Of course it does; where else could it commence? Fallen man can neither perceive his desperate need of salvation, nor come to Christ for it, till he has been renewed by the Holy Spirit.

"He hath made everything beautiful in his time" (Eccles. 3:11), and much of the beauty of God's spiritual handiwork is lost upon us unless we duly observe their "time." Has not the Spirit Himself emphasized this in the express enumeration He has given us in, "For whom he did foreknow, he also did predestinate to be conformed to the image of his Son, that he might be the firstborn among many brethren. Moreover, whom he did predestinate, them he also called; and whom he called, them he also justified; and whom he justified, them he also glorified" (Rom. 8:29-30). Verse 29 announces the divine foreordination; verse 30 states the manner of its actualization. It seems passing strange that with this divinely defined method before them, that so many preachers begin with our justification, instead of with that effectual call (from death unto life—our regeneration) which precedes it. Surely it is most obvious that regeneration must first take place in order to lay a foundation for our justification. Justification is by faith (Acts 13:39; Rom. 5:1; Gal. 3:8), and the sinner must be divinely quickened before he is capable of believing savingly.

Ah, does not the last statement made throw light upon and explain what we have said is so "passing strange"? Preachers today are so thoroughly imbued with free-willism that they have departed almost wholly from that sound evangelism which marked our forefathers. The radical difference between Arminianism and Calvinism is that the system of the former revolves about the creature, whereas the system of the latter has the Creator for the center of its orbit. The Arminian allots to man the first place, the Calvinist gives God that position of honor. Thus the Arminian begins his discussion of salvation with justification, for the sinner must *believe* before he can be forgiven; further back he will not go, for he is unwilling that man should be made *nothing* of. But the instructed Calvinist begins with election, descends to regeneration, and then shows that being born again (by the sovereign act of God, in which the creature has no part) the sinner is made capable of savingly believing the gospel.

Saved from the pleasure or love of sin. What multitudes of people would strongly resent being told that they delighted in evil! They would indignantly ask if we suppose them to be moral perverts? No indeed; a person may be thoroughly chaste and yet delight in evil. It may be that some of our own readers repudiate the charge that they have ever taken *pleasure* in sin, and would claim, on the contrary, that from earliest recollection they have detested wickedness in all its forms. Nor would we dare to call into question their sincerity; instead, we point out that it only affords another exemplification of the solemn fact that "the heart is *deceitful* above all things" (Jer. 17:9). But this is a matter that is not open to argument: the plain teaching of God's Word deciding the point once for all, and beyond its verdict there is no appeal. What, then, say the Scriptures?

So far from God's Word denying that there is any delight to be found therein, it expressly speaks of "the *pleasures* of sin," yet it immediately warns us that those pleasures are but "for a season" (Heb. 11:25), for the aftermath is painful and not pleasant; yea, unless God intervenes in His sovereign grace, they entail eternal torment. So, too, the Word refers to those who are "*lovers of pleasure* more than lovers of God" (II Tim. 3:4). It is indeed striking to observe how often this discordant note is struck in Scripture. It mentions those who "*love* vanity" (Ps. 4:2), "him that *loveth* violence" (Ps. 11:5), "thou *lovest evil* more than good" (Ps. 52:3), "he *loved* lies" (Ps. 109:17), "scorners *delight* in their scorning" (Prov. 1:22), "they which *delight in* their abominations" (Isa. 66:3), "their abominations were according as they *loved*" (Hos. 9:10), "who hated the good and *loved* the evil" (Mic. 3:2), "if any man *love* the world, the love of the Father is not in him" (I John 2:15). To love sin is far worse than to commit it, for a man may be suddenly tripped up or commit it through frailty.

The fact is, my reader, that we are not only born into this world with an evil nature, but with hearts that are thoroughly in love with sin. Sin is our native element. We are wedded to our lusts, and of ourselves are no more able to alter the bent of our corrupt nature than the Ethiopian can change his skin or the leopard his spots. But what is impossible with man is possible to God, and when He takes us in hand this is where He begins—by saving us from the pleasure or love of sin. This is the great miracle of grace, for the Almighty stoops down and picks up a loathsome leper from the dunghill, and makes him a new creature in Christ, so that the things he once loved he now hates, and the things he once hated he now loves. God commences by saving us from ourselves. He does not save us from the penalty of sin until He has delivered us from the love of sin.

And how is this miracle of grace accomplished, or rather, exactly *what does it consist of?* Negatively, not by eradicating the evil nature, nor even by refining it. Positively, by communicating a new nature, a holy nature, which loathes that which is evil and delights in all that is truly good. To be more specific: First, God saves His people from the pleasure or love of sin by putting His holy awe in their hearts, for "the fear of the Lord is to *hate* evil" (Prov. 8:13), and again, "the fear of the Lord is to *depart* from evil" (Prov. 6:16). Second, God saves His people from the pleasure of sin by communicating to them a new and vital principle: "the love of God is shed abroad in our hearts by the Holy Spirit" (Rom. 5:5), and where the love of God rules the heart, the love of sin is dethroned. Third, God saves His people from the love of sin by the Holy Spirit's drawing their affections unto things above, thereby taking them off the things which formerly enthralled them.

If on the one hand the unbeliever hotly denies that he is in love with sin, many a believer is often hard put to it to persuade himself that he *has been* saved from the love thereof. With an understanding that has been in part enlightened by the Holy Spirit, he is the better able to discern things in their true colors. With a heart that has been made honest by grace, he refuses to call bitter sweet. With a conscience that has been sensitized by the new birth, he the more quickly feels the workings of sin and the hankering of his affections for that which is forbidden. Moreover, the flesh remains in him, unchanged, and as the raven constantly craves carrion, so this corrupt principle in which our mothers conceived us, lusts after and delights in that which is the opposite of holiness. It is these things which occasion and give rise to the disturbing questions that clamor for answer within the genuine believer.

The sincere Christian is often made to seriously doubt if he *has been* delivered from the love of sin. Such questions as these painfully agitate his mind. Why do I so readily yield to temptation? Why do some of the vanities and pleasures of the world still possess so much attraction for me? Why do I chafe so much against any restraints being placed upon my lusts?

Why do I find the work of mortification so difficult and distasteful? Could such things as these be, if I were a new creature in Christ? Could such horrible experiences as these happen if God had saved me from taking pleasure in sin? Well do we know that we are here giving expression to the very doubts which exercise the minds of many of our readers, and those who are strangers thereto are to be pitied. But what shall we say in reply? How is this distressing problem to be resolved?

How may one be assured that he has been saved from the love of sin? Let us point out first that the presence of that within us which still lusts after and takes delight in some evil things, is *not incompatible* with our having been saved from the love of sin, paradoxical as that may sound. It is part of the mystery of the gospel that those who be saved are yet *sinners* in themselves. The point we are here dealing with is similar to and parallel with faith. The divine principle of faith in the heart does not cast out unbelief. Faith and doubts exist side by side within a quickened soul, which is evident from those words "Lord, I believe; help thou mine unbelief" (Mark 9:24). In like manner the Christian may exclaim and pray, "Lord, I long after holiness, help Thou my lustings after sin." And why is this? Because of the existence of two separate natures, the one at complete variance with the other within the Christian.

How, then, is the presence of faith to be ascertained? Not by the ceasings of unbelief, but by discovering *its own* fruits and works. Fruit may grow amid thorns—as flowers among weeds—yet it *is* fruit, nevertheless. Faith exists amid many doubts and fears. Notwithstanding opposing forces from within as well as from without us, faith still reaches out after God. Notwithstanding innumerable discouragements and defeats, faith continues to fight. Notwithstanding many refusals from God, it yet clings to Him, and says, "Except Thou bless me I will not let Thee go." Faith may be fearfully weak and fitful, often eclipsed by the clouds of unbelief; nevertheless the devil himself cannot persuade its possessor to repudiate God's Word, despise His Son, or abandon all hope. The presence of faith, then, may be ascertained in that it causes its possessor to come before God as an empty-handed beggar beseeching Him for mercy and blessing.

Now just as the presence of faith may be known amid all the workings of unbelief, so our salvation from the love of sin may be ascertained notwithstanding all the lustings of the flesh after that which is evil. But in what way? How is this initial aspect of salvation to be identified? We have already anticipated this question in an earlier paragraph, wherein we stated that God saved us from delighting in sin by imparting a nature that hates evil and loves holiness, which takes place at the new birth. Consequently, the real question to be settled is how may the Christian positively determine whether that new and holy nature has been imparted to him? The answer is, "By observing its activities, particularly the opposition it makes (under the energizings of the Holy Spirit) unto indwelling sin." Not only does the flesh (the principle of sin) lust against the spirit, but the spirit (the principle of holiness) lusts and wars against the flesh.

First, our salvation from the pleasure or love of sin may be recognized by sin's becoming a *burden* to us. This is truly a spiritual experience. Many souls are loaded with worldly anxieties, who know nothing of what it means to be bowed down with a sense of guilt. But when God takes us in hand, the iniquities and transgressions of our past life are made to lie as an intolerable load upon the conscience. When we are given a sight of ourselves as we appear before the eyes of the thrice holy God, we will exclaim with the psalmist, "For innumerable evils have compassed me about: mine iniquities have taken hold upon me, so that I am not able to look up; they are more than the hairs of mine head: therefore my heart faileth me" (40:12). So far from sin being pleasant, it is now felt as a cruel incubus, a crushing weight, an unendurable load. The soul is "heavy laden" (Matt. 11:28) and bowed down. A sense of guilt oppresses and the conscience cannot bear the weight upon it. Nor is this experience restricted to our first conviction; it continues with more or less acuteness throughout the Christian's life.

Second, our salvation from the pleasure of sin may be recognized by sin's becoming *bitter* to us. True, there are millions of the unregenerate who are filled with remorse over the harvest reaped from their sowing of wild oats. Yet that is not hatred of sin, but dislike of its consequences— ruined health, squandered opportunities, financial straitness, or social disgrace. No, what we have reference to is that anguish of heart which ever marks the one the Spirit takes in hand. When the veil of delusion is removed and we see sin in the light of God's countenance; when we are given a discovery of the depravity of our very nature, then we perceive that we are sunk in carnality and death. When sin is opened to us in all its secret workings, we are made to feel the vileness of our hypocrisy, self-righteousness, unbelief, impatience, and the utter filthiness of our hearts. And when the penitent soul views the sufferings of Christ, he can say with Job, "God maketh my heart soft" (23:16).

Ah, my reader, it is *this* experience which prepares the heart to go out after Christ: those who are whole need not a physician, but they who are quickened and convicted by the Spirit are anxious to be relieved by the great Physician. "The Lord killeth, and maketh alive; he bringeth down to the grave, and bringeth up. The Lord maketh poor, and maketh rich; he bringeth low, and lifteth up" (I Sam. 2:6-7). It is in this way that God slayeth our self-righteousness, maketh poor, and bringeth low—by making sin to be an intolerable burden and as bitter as wormwood to us. There can be no saving faith till the soul is filled with evangelical repentance, and repentance is a godly sorrow for sin, a holy detestation of sin, a sincere purpose to forsake it. The gospel calls upon men to repent of their sins, forsake their idols, and mortify their lusts, and thus it is utterly impossible for the gospel to be a message of glad tidings to those who are in love with sin and madly determined to perish rather than part with their idols.

Nor is this experience of sin's becoming bitter to us limited unto our first awakening—it continues, in varying degrees, to the end of our earthly pilgrimage. The Christian suffers under temptations, is pained by Satan's fiery assaults, and bleeds from the wounds inflicted by the evils he commits. It grieves him deeply that he makes such a wretched return unto God for His goodness, that he requites Christ so evilly for His dying love, that he responds so fitfully to the promptings of the Spirit. The wanderings of his mind when he desires to meditate upon the Word, the dullness of his heart when he seeks to pray, the worldly thoughts which invade his mind on the holy Sabbath, the coldness of his affections toward the Redeemer, cause him to groan daily; all of which goes to evidence that sin has been made bitter to him. He no longer welcomes those intruding thoughts which take his mind off God; rather does he sorrow over them. But "blessed are they that mourn: for they shall be comforted" (Matt. 5:4).

Third, our salvation from the pleasure of sin may be recognized by the felt *bondage* which sin produces. As it is not until a divine faith is planted in the heart that we become aware of our native and inveterate unbelief, so it is not until God saves us from the love of sin that we are conscious of the fetters it has placed around us. Then it is that we discover we are "without strength," unable to do anything pleasing to God, incapable of running the race set before us. A divinely drawn picture of the saved soul's felt bondage is to be found in Romans 7: "For I know that in me (that is, in my flesh) dwelleth no good thing: for to will is present with me, but how to perform that which is good I find not. For the good that I would, I do not; but the evil which I would not, that I do. . . . For I delight in the law of God after the inward man: but I see another law in my members, warring against the law of my mind, and bringing me into captivity to the law of sin" (vv. 18-19, 22-23). And what is the sequel? This, the agonizing cry, "O wretched man that I am! who shall deliver me from the body of this death." If *that* be the sincere lamentation of your heart, then God has saved *you* from the pleasure of sin.

Let it be pointed out, though, that salvation from the love of sin is felt and evidenced in varying degrees by different Christians, and at different periods in the life of the same Christian, according to the measure of grace which God bestows, and according as that grace is active and operative. Some seem to have a more intense hatred of sin in all its forms than do others, yet the principle of hating sin is found in all real Christians. Some Christians, rarely if ever, commit any deliberate and premeditated sins; more often they are tripped up, suddenly tempted (to be angry or to tell a lie), and are overcome. But with others the case is quite otherwise: they—fearful to say—actually plan evil acts. If anyone indignantly denies that such a thing is possible in a saint, and insists that such a character is a stranger to saving grace, we would remind him of David: was not the murder of Uriah definitely planned? This second class of Christians finds it doubly hard to believe they have been saved from the love of sin.

19 Salvation From the Penalty of Sin

This follows upon our regeneration which is evidenced by evangelical repentance and unfeigned faith. Every soul that truly puts his trust in the Lord Jesus Christ is then and there saved from the penalty—the guilt, the wages, the punishment—of sin. When the apostles said to the penitent jailor, "Believe on the Lord Jesus Christ and thou shalt be saved," they signified that all his sins would be remitted by God; just as when the Lord said to the poor woman, "Thy faith hath saved thee: go in peace" (Luke 7:50). He meant that all her sins were now forgiven her, for forgiveness has to do with the criminality and punishment of sin. To the same effect when we read, "By grace are ye saved through faith" (Eph. 2:8), it is to be understood that the Lord has actually "delivered us from the wrath to come" (I Thess. 1:10).

This aspect of our salvation is to be contemplated from two separate viewpoints: the divine and the human. The divine side of it is found in the mediatorial office and work of Christ, who as the Sponsor and Surety of His people met the requirements of the law on their behalf, working out for them a perfect righteousness and enduring Himself the curse and condemnation which was due them, consummated at the cross. It was there that He was "wounded for our transgressions and bruised for our iniquities" (Isa. 53:5). It was there that He, judicially, "his own self bear our sins in his own body on the tree" (I Peter 2:24). It was there that He was "smitten of God and afflicted" while He was making atonement for the offenses of His people. Because Christ suffered in my stead, I go free; because He died, I live; because He was forsaken of God, I am reconciled to Him. This is the great marvel of grace, which will evoke ceaseless praise from the redeemed throughout eternity.

The human side of our salvation from the penalty of sin respects our repentance and faith. Though these possess no merits whatever, and though they in no sense purchase our pardon, yet, according to the order which God has appointed, they are (instrumentally) essential, for salvation does not become ours experimentally until they are exercised. Repentance is the hand releasing those filthy objects it had previously clung to so tenaciously; faith is extending an empty hand to God to receive the gift of His grace. Repentance is a godly sorrow for sin; faith is accepting God's pardon thereof. Repentance is crying, "God be merciful to me the sinner"; faith is receiving the sinner's Saviour. Repentance is revulsion of the filth and pollution of sin; faith is seeking cleansing therefrom. Repentance is the sinner covering his mouth and crying, "Unclean, unclean!"; faith is the leper coming to Christ and saying, "Lord, if thou wilt, thou canst make me clean."

So far from repentance and faith being meritorious graces, they are self-emptying ones. The one who truly repents takes his place as a lost sinner before God, confessing himself to be a guilty wretch deserving naught but unsparing judgment at the hands of divine justice. Faith looks away from corrupt and ruined self, and views the amazing provision which God has made for such a hell-deserving creature. Faith lays hold of the Son of God's love, as a drowning man clutches at a passing spar. Faith surrenders to the Lordship of Christ and gladly owns His right to reign over him. Faith rests upon the promises of God, setting to its seal that He is true. The moment the soul surrenders itself to the Lordship of Christ, rests upon the merits and efficacy of His sacrifice, his sins are removed from God's sight "as far as the east is from the west"; he is now eternally saved from the wrath to come.

We cannot do better here than quote those sublime lines of Augustus Toplady:

> From whence this fear and unbelief?
> Hast Thou, O Father, put to grief
>   Thy spotless Son for me?
> And will the righteous Judge of men
> Condemn me for that debt of sin
>   Which, Lord, was laid on Thee?
>
> If Thou hast my discharge procured,
> And freely in my place endured
>   The whole of wrath divine;
> Payment God cannot twice demand,
> First at my bleeding Surety's hand,
>   And then again at mine.
>
> Complete atonement Thou hast made,
> And to the utmost farthing paid,

Whate'er Thy people owed;
How then can wrath on me take place,
If sheltered in Thy righteousness,
And sprinkled with Thy blood?

Turn, then, my soul, unto thy rest,
The merits of thy great High Priest
Speak peace and liberty:
Trust in His efficacious blood,
Nor fear thy banishment from God,
Since Jesus died for thee.

While deliverance from the love of sin has to do entirely with the experimental side of our salvation, remission of the penalty of sin concerns the legal aspect only, or in other words, the believer's *justification*. Justification is a forensic term and has to do with the law courts, for it is the decision or verdict of the judge. Justification is the opposite of condemnation. Condemnation means that a man has been charged with a crime, his guilt is established, and accordingly the law pronounces upon him sentence of punishment. On the contrary, justification means that the accused is found to be guiltless, the law has nothing against him, and therefore he is acquitted and exonerated, leaving the court without a stain upon his character. When we read in Scripture that believers are "justified from all things" (Acts 13:39), it signifies that their case has been tried in the high court of heaven and that God, the Judge of all the earth, has acquitted them: "There is therefore now *no* condemnation to them which are in Christ Jesus" (Rom. 8:1).

But to be without condemnation is only the negative side: justification means to declare or pronounce righteous—up to the law's requirements. Justification implies that the law has been fulfilled, obeyed, magnified, for nothing short of this would meet the just demands of God. Hence, as His people, fallen in Adam, were unable to measure up to the divine standard, God appointed that His own Son should become incarnate, be the Surety of His people, and answer the demands of the law in their stead. Here, then, is the sufficient answer which may be made to the two objections which unbelief is ready to raise: how can God acquit the guilty? How can He declare righteous one who is devoid of righteousness? Bring in the Lord Jesus and all difficulty disappears! The guilt of our sins was imputed or legally transferred to *Him*, so that He suffered the full penalty of what was due them; the merits of His obedience is imputed or legally transferred to *us*, so that we stand before God in all the acceptableness of our Sponsor (Rom. 5:18-19; II Cor. 5:21, etc.). Not only has the law nothing against us, but we are entitled to its reward.

20 Salvation From the Power of Sin

This is a present and protracted process, and is as yet incomplete. It is the most difficult part of our subject, and upon it the greatest confusion of thought prevails, especially among young Christians. Many there are who, having learned that the Lord Jesus is the Saviour of sinners, have jumped to the erroneous conclusion that if they but exercise faith in Him, surrender to His Lordship, commit their souls into His keeping, He will remove their corrupt nature and destroy their evil propensities. But after they have really trusted in Him, they discover that evil is still present with them, that their hearts are still deceitful above all things and desperately wicked, and that no matter how they strive to resist temptation, pray for overcoming grace, and use the means of God's appointing, they seem to grow worse and worse instead of better, until they seriously doubt if they are saved at all. They are now *being saved!*

Even when a person has been regenerated and justified the flesh or corrupt nature remains within him and ceaselessly harasses him. Yet this ought not to perplex him. To the saints at Rome Paul said, "Let not sin therefore reign in your mortal body" (6:12), which would be entirely meaningless had sin been eradicated from them. Writing to the Corinthian saints he said, "Having therefore these promises, dearly beloved, let us cleanse ourselves from all filthiness of the flesh and spirit, perfecting holiness in the fear of God" (II Cor. 7:1); obviously such an exhortation is needless if sin has been purged from our beings. "Humble yourselves therefore under the mighty hand of God, that he may exalt you in due time" (I Peter 5:6); what need have Christians for such a word as this, except pride still lurks and works within them? But all room for controversy on this point is excluded if we bow to that inspired declaration, "If we say we have no sin we deceive ourselves, and the truth is not in us" (I John 1:8).

The old carnal nature remains in the believer: he is still a *sinner,* though a saved one. What, then, is the young Christian to do? Is he powerless?

Must he resort to stoicism, and make up his mind that there is naught but a life of defeat before him? Certainly not! The first thing for him to do is to learn thoroughly the humiliating truth that in himself he is "without strength." It was here that Israel failed; when Moses made known to them the Law, they boastfully declared, "All that the Lord hath said we will do and be obedient" (Exod. 24:7). Ah! how little did they realize that "in the flesh there dwelleth no good thing." It was here, too, that Peter failed: he was self-confident and boasted that "though all men be offended because of thee, yet will I never be offended . . . though I should die with thee, yet will I not deny thee"—how little he knew his own heart. This complacent spirit lurks within each of us. So long as we cherish the belief that we can "do better next time" it is evident that we still have confidence in our own powers. Not until we heed the Saviour's word "without me ye can do nothing" do we take the first step toward victory. Only when we are weak (in ourselves) are we strong.

The believer still has the carnal nature within him, and he has no strength in himself to check its evil propensities, nor to overcome its sinful solicitations. But the believer in Christ also has another nature within him, which is received at the new birth: "that which is born of the Spirit is spirit" (John 3:6). The believer, then, has two natures within him: one which is sinful, the other spiritual. These two natures being totally different in character, are antagonistic to each other. To this antagonism or conflict the apostle referred when he said, "The flesh lusteth against the spirit, and the spirit against the flesh" (Gal. 5:17). Now *which* of these two natures is to regulate the believer's life? It is manifest that both cannot, for they are contrary to each other. It is equally evident that the stronger of the two will exert the more controlling power. It is also clear that in the young Christian the carnal nature is the stronger, because he was born with it, and hence it has many years start of the spiritual nature, which he did not receive until he was born again.

Further, it is unnecessary to argue at length that the only way by which we can strengthen and develop the new nature is by *feeding* it. In every realm growth is dependent upon food, suitable food, daily food. The nourishment which God has provided for our spiritual nature is found in His own Word, for "Man shall not live by bread alone, but by every word that proceedeth out of the mouth of God" (Matt. 4:4). It is to this that Peter has reference when he says, "As new-born babes desire the sincere [pure] milk of the word, that ye may grow thereby" (I Peter 2:2). In proportion as we feed upon the heavenly Manna, such will be our spiritual growth. Of course, there are other things beside food needful to growth: we must breathe, and in a pure atmosphere. This, translated into spiritual terms, signifies *prayer*. It is when we approach the throne of grace and meet our Lord face to face, that our spiritual lungs are filled with the ozone of heaven. *Exercise* is another essential to growth, and this finds it accomplishment in walking with the Lord. If, then, we heed these primary laws of spiritual health, the new nature will flourish.

But not only must the new nature be fed, it is equally necessary for our spiritual well-being that the old nature should be starved. This is what the apostle had in mind when he said, "Make not provision for the flesh, unto the lusts thereof" (Rom. 13:14). To starve the old nature, to "make not provision for the flesh," means that we abstain from everything that would stimulate our carnality; that we avoid, as we would a plague, all that is calculated to prove injurious to our spiritual welfare. Not only must we deny ourselves the "pleasures of sin," shun such things as the saloon, theater, dance, card table, etc., but we must separate ourselves from worldly companions, cease to read worldly literature, abstain from everything upon which we cannot ask God's blessing. Our affections are to be set upon things above, and not upon things on the earth (Col. 3:2). Does this seem a high standard, and sound impracticable? Holiness in all things is that at which we are to aim, and failure so to do explains the *leanness* of so many Christians. Let the young believer realize that whatever does not help his spiritual life hinders it.

Here then, in brief, is the answer to our question, "What is the young Christian to do in order for deliverance from indwelling sin?" It is true that we are still in this world, but we are not "of" it (John 17:14). It is true that we are forced to associate with godless people, but this is ordained of God in order that we may "let our light so shine before men that they may see our good works, and glorify our Father which is in heaven" (Matt. 5:16). There is a wide difference between associating with sinners as we go about our daily tasks, and making them our intimate companions and friends. Only as we feed upon the Word can we "grow in grace and in the knowledge of our Lord Jesus Christ" (II Peter 3:18). Only as we starve the old nature can we expect deliverance from its power and pollution. Then let us earnestly heed that exhortation, "Put ye off concerning the former conversation [behavior] the old man, which is corrupt according to the deceitful lusts, and be renewed in the spirit of your mind, and that ye put on the new man, which, after God, is created in righteousness and true holiness" (Eph. 4:22-24).

Above, we have dealt only with the *human* side of the problem as to how to obtain deliverance from the dominion of sin. Necessarily there is a *divine* side too. It is only by God's grace that we are enabled to use the means which He has provided for us, as it is only by the power of His Spirit who dwells within us that we can "lay aside every weight, and the sin which doth so easily beset us, and run with patience the race that is set before us" (Heb. 12:1). These two aspects (the divine and human) are brought together in a number of Scriptures. We are bidden to "work out our own salvation with fear and trembling," but the apostle immediately added, "For it is God which worketh in you both to will and to do of his good pleasure" (Phil. 2:12-13). Thus, we are to work out that which God has wrought within us; in other words, if we walk in the Spirit we shall not fulfill the lusts of the flesh (Gal. 5:16). It has now been shown that salvation from the power of sin is a *process* which goes on throughout the believer's life. It is to this Solomon referred when he said, "The path of the just is as the shining light, which shineth *more and more* unto the perfect day" (Prov. 4:18).

As our salvation from the pleasure of sin is the consequence of our regeneration, and as salvation from the penalty of sin respects our justification, so salvation from the power of sin has to do with the practical side of our sanctification. The word *sanctification* signifies "separation"—separation from sin. We need hardly say that the word *holiness* is strictly synonymous with sanctification, being an alternative rendering of the same Greek word. As the practical side of sanctification has to do with our separation from sin, we are told, "Let us cleanse ourselves from all filthiness of the flesh and spirit, perfecting holiness in the fear of God" (II Cor. 7:1). That practical sanctification or holiness is a process, a progressive experience, is clear from this: "Follow . . . holiness, without which no man shall see the Lord" (Heb. 12:14). The fact that we are exhorted to "follow" holiness clearly intimates that we have not yet attained unto the divine standard which God requires of us. This is further seen in the passage just quoted above: "perfecting holiness" or completing it.

We must now enter into a little fuller detail upon *the divine side* of our salvation from the power and pollution of sin. When a sinner truly receives Christ as his Lord and Saviour, God does not then and there take him to heaven. On the contrary, he is likely to be left down here for many years, and this world is a place of *danger,* for it lieth in the wicked one (I John 5:19) and all pertaining to it is opposed to the Father (I John 2:16). Therefore, the believer needs daily salvation from this hostile system. Accordingly we read that Christ "gave himself for our sins, that he might deliver us from this present evil world, according to the will of God our Father" (Gal. 1:4). Not only is the sinner not taken to heaven when he first savingly believes, but, as we have seen, the evil nature is not taken out of him; nevertheless God does not leave him completely under its dominion, but graciously delivers him from its regal power. He uses a great variety of means in accomplishing this.

A. *By granting us a clearer view of our inward depravity,* so that we are made to abhor ourselves. By nature we are thoroughly in love with ourselves, but as the divine work of grace is carried forward in our souls we come to loathe ourselves; and that, my reader, is a very distressing experience—one which is conveniently shelved by most of our modern preachers.

The concept which many young Christians form from preachers is that the experience of a genuine believer is a smooth, peaceful, and joyous one; but he soon discovers that this is not verified in his personal history, but rather it is completely falsified. And this staggers him! Supposing the preacher to know more about such matters than himself, he is now filled with disturbing doubts about his very salvation, and the devil promptly tells him he is only a hypocrite, and never was saved at all.

Only those who have actually passed through or are passing through this painful experience have any real conception thereof; there is as much difference between an actual acquaintance with it and the mere reading a description of it, as there is between personally visiting a country and examining it first hand and simply studying a map of it. But how are we to account for one who has been saved from the pleasure and penalty of sin, now being made increasingly conscious not only of its polluting presence but of its tyrannizing power? How explain the fact that the Christian now finds himself growing worse and worse, and the more closely he endeavors to walk with God, the more he finds the flesh bringing forth its horrible works in ways it had not done previously? The answer is because of increased light from God, by which he now discovers filth of which he was previously unawares—the sun shining into a neglected room does not create the dust and cobwebs, it simply reveals them.

Thus it is with the Christian. The more the light of the Spirit is turned upon him inwardly, the more he discovers the horrible plague of his heart (I Kings 8:38), and the more he realizes what a wretched failure he is. The fact is, dear discouraged soul, that the more you are growing out of love with yourself, the more you are being saved from the power of sin. Wherein lies its fearful potency? Why, in its power to *deceive* us. It lies to us. It did so to Adam and Eve. It gives us false estimates of values so that we mistake the tinsel for real gold. To be saved from the power of sin, is to have our eyes opened so that we see things in God's light: it is to know the *truth* about things all around us, and the truth about ourselves. Satan has blinded the minds of them that believe not, but the Holy Spirit hath shined in our hearts "unto the light of the knowledge of the glory of God in the face of Jesus Christ" (II Cor. 4:4, 6).

But further: sin not only deceives, it *puffs up*, causing its infatuated victims to think highly of themselves. As I Timothy 3:6 tells us, to be "lifted up with pride" is to "fall into the condemnation of the devil." Ah, it was insane egotism which caused him to say, "I will ascend into heaven, I will exalt my throne above the stars of God: I will sit also upon the mount of the congregation, in the sides of the north. I will ascend above the heights of the clouds: I will be like the Most High" (Isa. 14:13-14). Is there any wonder, then, that those in whom he works are filled with pride and complacency! Sin ever produces self-love and self-righteousness: the most abandoned of characters will tell you, "I know that I am weak, yet I have a good heart." But when God takes us in hand, it is the very opposite: the working of the Spirit subdues our pride. How? By giving increasing discoveries of self and of the exceeding sinfulness of sin, so that each one cries with Job, "Behold! I am vile" (40:4). Such an one is being saved from the power of sin—its power to deceive and to inflate.

B. *By sore chastenings.* This is another means which God uses in delivering His people from sin's dominion. "We have had fathers of our flesh which corrected us, and we gave them reverence: shall we not much rather be in subjection unto the Father of spirits, and live? For they verily for a few days chastened us after their own pleasure: but he for our profit, that we might be partakers of his holiness" (Heb. 12:9-10). Those chastenings assume varied forms: sometimes they are external, sometimes internal, but whatever be their nature they are painful to flesh and blood. Sometimes these divine chastisements are of long duration, and then the soul is apt to ask, "Why standest thou afar off, O Lord? Why dost thou hide thyself in times of trouble?" (Ps. 10:1), for it seems as though God has deserted us. Earnest prayer is made for a mitigation of suffering, but no relief is granted; grace is earnestly sought for meekly bowing to the rod, but unbelief, impatience, rebellion, seem to wax stronger and stronger, and the soul is hard put to it to believe in God's love; but as Hebrews 12:11 tells us, "Now no chastening for the present seemeth to be joyous, but grievous; nevertheless, afterward it yieldeth the peaceful fruit of righteousness unto them which are exercised thereby."

This life is a schooling, and chastenings are one of the chief methods God employs in the training of His children. Sometimes they are sent for the *correcting* of our faults, and therefore we must pray, "Cause me to understand wherein I have erred" (Job 6:24). Let us steadily bear in mind that it is the "rod" and not the sword which is smiting us, held in the hand of our loving Father and not the avenging Judge. Sometimes they are sent for the *prevention of sin,* as Paul was given a thorn in the flesh "lest he should be exalted above measure, through the abundance of the revelations" given him. Sometimes they are sent for our spiritual *education,* that by them we may be brought to a deeper experiential acquaintance with God: "It is good for me that I have been afflicted, that I might learn thy statutes" (Ps. 119:71). Sometimes they are sent for the testing and strengthening of our *graces:* "We glory in tribulations also: knowing that tribulation worketh patience; and patience, experience; and experience, hope" (Rom. 5:3-4); "Count it all joy when ye fall into varied trials: knowing this, that the trying of your faith worketh patience" (James 1:2-3).

Chastening is God's *sin-purging medicine,* sent to wither our fleshly aspirations, to detach our hearts from carnal objects, to deliver us from our idols, to wean us more thoroughly from the world. God has bidden us, "Be not unequally yoked together with unbelievers . . . come out from among them, and be ye separate" (II Cor. 6:14, 17); and we are slow to respond and, therefore, He takes measures to *drive us out.* He has bidden us "love not the world," and if we disobey we must not be surprised if He causes some of our worldly friends to hate and persecute us. God has bidden us "mortify ye therefore your members which are upon the earth" (Col. 3:5); if we refuse to comply with this unpleasant task, then we may expect God Himself to use the pruning knife upon us. God has bidden us "cease ye from man" (Isa. 2:22), and if we will trust our fellows, we are made to suffer for it.

"Despise not thou the chastening of the Lord, nor faint when thou art rebuked of him" (Heb. 12:5). This is a salutary warning. So far from despising it, we should be grateful that God cares so much and takes such trouble with us, and that His bitter physic produces such healthful effects. "In their affliction they will seek me early" (Hos. 5:15)—while everything is running smoothly for us, we are apt to be self-sufficient; but when trouble comes, we promptly turn unto the Lord. Own, then, with the psalmist, "In faithfulness thou hast afflicted me" (119:75). Not only do God's chastisements, when sanctified to us, subdue the workings of pride and wean us more from the world, but they make the divine promises more precious to the heart. Then such as this takes on a new meaning, "When thou passest through the waters, I will be with thee, . . . when thou walkest through the fire, thou shalt not be burned" (Isa. 43:2). Moreover, they break down selfishness and make us more sympathetic to our fellow sufferers: "Who comfortest us in all our tribulation, that we may be able to comfort them which are in any trouble" (II Cor. 1:4).

C. *By bitter disappointments.* God has plainly warned us that "all is vanity and vexation of spirit, and there is no profit under the sun" (Eccles. 2:11), and that by one who was permitted to gratify the physical senses as none other ever has been. Yet we do not take this warning to heart, for we do not really believe it. On the contrary, we persuade ourselves that satisfaction *is to be found* in things under the sun, that the creature *can* give contentment to our hearts. As well attempt to fill a circle with a square! The heart was made for *God,* and He alone can meet its needs. But by nature we are idolators, putting things into His place. Those things we invest with qualities they possess not, and sooner or later our delusions are rudely exposed to us, and we discover that the images in our minds are only dreams, that our golden idol is but clay after all.

God so orders His providences that our earthly nest is destroyed. The winds of adversity compel us to leave the downy bed of carnal ease and luxuriation. Grievous losses are experiences in some form or other. Trusted friends prove fickle, and in the hour of need fail us. The family circle, which had so long sheltered us and where peace and happiness was found, is broken up by the grim hand of death. Health fails and weary nights are our portion. These trying experiences, these bitter disappointments, are another of the means which our gracious God employs to save us from the pleasure and pollution of sin. By them He discovers to us the vanity and vexation of the creature. By them He weans us more completely from the world. By them He teaches us that the objects in which we sought refreshment are but "broken cisterns," and this that we may turn to *Christ* and draw from Him who is the well of living water, the One who alone can supply true satisfaction of soul.

It is in this way we are experimentally taught to look off from the present to the future, for our rest is not here. "For we are *saved by hope:* but hope that is seen is not hope: for what a man seeth, why doth he yet hope for?" (Rom. 8:24). Let it be duly noted that this comes immediately after "we ourselves groan within ourselves." Thus to be "saved by hope" respects our present salvation from the power of sin. Complete salvation is now the Christian's only in title and expectation. It is not here said that we "*shall* be saved by hope," but "we *are* saved by hope"—that hope which looks for the fulfilling of God's promises. Hope has to do with a future good, with something which as yet "is seen not": we "hope" not for something which is already enjoyed. Herein hope differs from faith. Faith, as it is an assent, is in the mind; but hope is seated in the affections, stirred by the desirability of the things promised.

And, my reader, the bitter disappointments of life are naught but a dark background upon which hope may shine forth the more brightly. Christ does not immediately take to heaven the one who puts his trust in Him. No, He keeps him here upon earth for a while to be exercised and tried. While he is awaiting his complete blessedness there is such a difference between him and it, and he encounters many difficulties and trials. Not having yet received his inheritance, there is need and occasion of hope, for only by its exercise can things future be sought after. The stronger our hope, the more earnestly shall we be engaged in the pursuit of it. We have to be weaned from present things in order for the heart to be fixed upon a future good.

D. *By the gift of the Spirit and His operations within us.* God's great gift of Christ for us is matched by the gift of the Spirit in us, for we owe as much to the One as we do to the Other. The new nature in the Christian is powerless apart from the Spirit's daily renewing. It is by His gracious operations that we have discovered to us the nature and extent of sin, are made to strive against it, are brought to grieve over it. It is by the Spirit that faith, hope, prayer, is kept alive within the soul. It is by the Spirit we are moved to use the means of grace which God has appointed for our spiritual preservation and growth. It is by the Spirit that sin is prevented from having complete dominion over us, for, as the result of His indwelling us, there is something else beside sin in the believer's heart and life, namely, the fruits of holiness and righteousness.

To sum up this aspect of our subject: Salvation from the power of indwelling sin is not the taking of the evil nature out of the believer in this life, nor by effecting any improvement in it. "That which is born of the flesh is flesh" (John 3:6) and it remains so, unchanged to the end. Nor is it by the Spirit so subduing indwelling sin that it is rendered less active, for the flesh not merely lusts, but "lusteth [ceaselessly] against the spirit"—it never sleeps, not even when our bodies do, as our dreams evidence. No, and in some form or other, the flesh is constantly producing its evil works. It may not be in external acts, seen by the eyes of our fellows, but certainly so internally, in things seen by God—such as covetousness, discontent, pride, unbelief, self-will, ill-will toward others, and a hundred other evils. No, none is saved from *sinning* in this life.

Present salvation from the power of sin consists in, first, delivering us from the *love* of it, which though begun at our regeneration is continued throughout our practical sanctification. Second, from its *blinding delusiveness,* so that it can no more deceive as once it did. Third, from our *excusing* it: "That which I do, I allow not" (Rom. 7:15). This is one of the surest marks of regeneration. In the fullest sense of the word the believer "allows" it not *before* he sins, for every real Christian when in his right mind desires to be wholly kept from sinning. He "allows" it not fully *when doing it,* for in the actual committing thereof there is an inward reserve—the new nature consents not. He "allows" it not *afterwards,* as Psalm 51 evidences so plainly of the case of David.

The force of this word "allow" in Romans 7:15 may be seen from "truly ye bear witness that *ye allow* the deeds of your fathers: for they killed them [the prophets] and ye build their sepulchres" (Luke 11:48). So far from those Jews being ashamed of their fathers and abhorring their wicked conduct, they erected a monument to their honor. Thus, to "allow" is the opposite of to be ashamed of and sorrow over: it is to condone and vindicate. Therefore, when it is said that the believer "allows not" the evil of which he is guilty, it means that he seeks not to justify himself or throw the blame on someone else, as both Adam and Eve did. That the Christian allows not sin is evident by his shame over it, his sorrow for it, his confession of it, his loathing himself because of it, his renewed resolution to forsake it.

21 Salvation From the Presence of Sin

We now turn to that aspect of our subject which has to do solely with the future. Sin is yet to be completely eradicated from the believer's being, so that he shall appear before God without any spot or blemish. True, this is his legal status even now, yet it has not become so in his state or experience. As God views the believer in Christ, he appears before Him in all the excellency of his Sponsor; but as God views him as he yet is in himself (and that he *does* do so is proved by His chastenings), he beholds all the ruin which the Fall has wrought in him. But this will not always be the case: no, blessed be His name, the Lord is reserving the best wine for the last. And even now we have tasted that He is gracious, but the fullness of His grace will only be entered into and enjoyed by us after this world is left behind.

Those Scriptures which present our salvation as a *future prospect* are all concerned with our final deliverance from the very inbeing of sin. To this Paul referred when he said, "Now is our salvation nearer than when we believed" (Rom. 13:11)—not our salvation from the pleasure, the penalty, or the power of sin, but from its very presence. "For our citizenship is in heaven: from whence we also look for *the Saviour,* the Lord Jesus Christ" (Phil. 3:20). Yes, it is the "Saviour" we await, for it is at His return that the whole election of grace shall enter into their full salvation; as it is written, "Unto them that look for him shall he appear the second time without sin unto *salvation*" (Heb. 9:28). In like manner, when another apostle declares, "We are kept by the power of God through faith unto salvation, ready to be revealed in the last time" (I Peter 1:5), he has reference to this grand consummation of the believer's salvation, when he shall be forever rid of the very presence of sin.

Our salvation from the pleasure of sin is effected by Christ's taking up His abode in our hearts: "Christ liveth in me" (Gal. 2:20). Our salvation from the penalty of sin was secured by Christ's sufferings on the cross, where He endured the punishment due our iniquities. Our salvation from the power of sin is obtained by the gracious operations of the Spirit which Christ sends to His people—therefore is He designated "the Spirit of Christ" (Rom. 8:9; cf. Gal. 4:6; Rev. 3:1). Our salvation from the presence of sin will be accomplished at Christ's second advent: "For our citizenship is in heaven, from whence also we look for the Saviour, the Lord Jesus Christ: who shall change our vile body that it may be fashioned like unto his glorious body, according to the working whereby he is able even to subdue all things unto himself" (Phil. 3:20-21). And again we are told, "We know that when he shall appear, we shall be like him, for we shall see him as he is" (I John 3:2). It is all of *Christ* from beginning to end.

Man was originally created in the image and likeness of God, reflecting the moral perfections of his Maker. But sin came in and he fell from his pristine glory, and by that fall God's image in him was broken and His likeness marred. But in the redeemed that image is to be restored; yea, they are to be granted a far higher honor than that bestowed upon the first Adam: they are to be made like the last Adam. It is written, "For whom he did foreknow, he also did predestinate to be conformed to the image of his Son, that he might be the firstborn among many brethren" (Rom. 8:29). This blessed purpose of God in our predestination will not be fully realized until the second coming of our Lord: then it will be that His people shall be completely emancipated from the thralldom and corruption of sin. Then shall Christ "present it to himself a *glorious* church, not having spot or wrinkle, or any such thing; but that it should be holy and without blemish" (Eph. 5:27).

Salvation from the pleasure or love of sin takes place at our *regeneration;* salvation from the penalty or punishment of sin occurs at our *justification;* salvation from the power or dominion of sin is accomplished during our practical *sanctification;* salvation from the presence or inbeing of sin is consummated at our *glorification:* "Whom he justified, them he also glorified" (Rom. 8:30). Not so much is revealed in Scripture on this fourth aspect of our subject, for God's Word was not given us to gratify curiosity. Yet sufficient *is* made known to feed faith, strengthen hope, draw out love, and make us "run with patience the race that is set before us." In our present state we are incapable of forming any real conception of the bliss awaiting us: yet as Israel's spies brought back the bunch of "the grapes of Eschol" as a sample of the good things to be found in the land of Canaan, so the Christian is granted a foretaste and earnest of his inheritance on high.

"Till we all come in the unity of the faith, and of the knowledge of the Son of God, to a perfect man, unto the measure of the stature of the fulness of Christ" (Eph. 4:13). It is to the image of a glorified Christ that we are predestinated to be conformed. Behold Him on the mount of transfiguration, when a foreview of His glory was granted the favored disciples. Such is the dazzling splendor of His person that Saul of Tarsus was temporarily blinded by a glimpse of it, and the beloved John in the isle of Patmos "fell at his feet as dead" (Rev. 1:17) when he beheld Him. That which awaits us can best be estimated as it is contemplated in the light of God's wondrous *love*. The portion which Christ Himself has received, is the expression of God's love for Him; and, as the Saviour has assured His people concerning His Father's love unto them "and hast loved them as thou lovest me" (John 17:23), and therefore, as He promised "where I am, there ye may be also" (John 14:3).

But is not the believer forever done with sin *at death?* Yes, thank God, such is the case; yet that is not his *glorification,* for his body goes to corruption, and that is the effect of sin. But it is written of the believer's body, "It is sown in corruption, it is raised in incorruption; it is sown in dishonor, it is raised in glory; it is sown in weakness, it is raised in power; it is sown a natural body, it is raised a spiritual body" (I Cor. 15:42-44). Nevertheless, at death itself the Christian's soul is entirely freed from the presence of sin. This is clear from "Blessed are the dead which die in the Lord from henceforth, yea, saith the Spirit, that they may rest from their labours; and their works do follow them" (Rev. 14:13). What is signified by "that they may rest from their labours"? Why, something more blessed than ceasing from earning their daily bread by the sweat of their brows, for that will be true of the unsaved also. Those who die in the Lord rest from their "labours" *with sin:* their painful conflicts with indwelling corruption, Satan, and the world. The fight which faith now wages is then ended, and full relief from sin is theirs forever.

22 Summary

The fourfold salvation from sin of the Christian was strikingly typified in God's dealings with the nation of Israel of old. First, we have a vivid portrayal of their deliverance from the *pleasure* or love of sin: "And the children of Israel sighed by reason of the bondage, and they cried, and their cry came up unto God by reason of the bondage. And God heard their groaning" (Exod. 2:23-24). What a contrast does that present from what we read of in the closing chapters of Genesis! There we hear the king of Egypt saying to Joseph, "The land of Egypt is before thee: in *the best of* the land make thy father and brethren to dwell; in the land of Goshen" (47:6). Accordingly we are told, "And Israel dwelt in the land of Egypt, in the country of Goshen; and they had possessions therein, and grew and multiplied exceedingly" (47:27). Now Egypt is the Old Testament symbol of the world, as a system opposed to God. And it was there, in the "best part" of it, the descendants of Abraham had settled. But the Lord had designs of mercy and something far better for them: yet before they could appreciate Canaan they had to be weaned from Egypt. Hence we find them in cruel bondage there, smarting under the lash of the taskmasters. In this way they were made to loathe Egypt and long for deliverance therefrom. The theme of Exodus is *redemption:* how striking, then, to see that God *begins* His work of redemption by making His people to groan and cry out under their bondage! The portion Christ bestows is not welcome till we are made sick of this world.

Second, in Exodus 12 we have a picture of God's people being delivered from the *penalty* of sin. On the Passover night the angel of death came and slew all the firstborn of the Egyptians. But why spare the firstborn of the Israelites? Not because they were guiltless before God, for all had sinned and come short of His glory. The Israelites, equally with the Egyptians, were guilty in His sight, and deserving of unsparing judgment. It was at this very point that the grace of God came in and met their need. Another was slain in their room and died in their stead. An innocent victim was killed and its blood shed, pointing to the coming of "the Lamb of God which taketh away the sin of the world." The head of each Israelitish household sprinkled the lamb's blood on the lintel and posts of his door, and hence the firstborn in it was spared from the avenging angel: God promised, "When I see the blood I will pass over you" (Exod. 12:13). Thus, Israel was saved from the penalty of sin by means of the lamb dying in their stead.

Third, Israel's wilderness journey adumbrated the believer's salvation from the *power* of sin. Israel did not enter Canaan immediately upon their exodus from Egypt: they had to face the temptations and trials of the desert where they spent not less than forty years. But what a gracious and full provision did God make for His people! Manna was given them daily from heaven—figure of that food which God's Word now supplies for our spiritual nourishment. Water was given from the smitten rock—emblem of the Holy Spirit sent by the smitten Christ to dwell within us (John 7:38-39). A cloud and a pillar of fire guided them by day and guarded them by night, reminding us of how God directs our steps and shields us from our foes. Best of all, Moses, their great leader, was with them, counseling, admonishing, and interceding for them—figure of the Captain of our salvation: "Lo, I am with you alway."

Fourth, the actual entrance of Israel into the promised land foreshadowed the believer's glorification, when he enters into the full enjoyment of that possession which Christ has purchased for him. The experiences Israel met with in Canaan have a double typical significance. From one viewpoint they presaged the conflict which faith encounters while the believer is left upon earth, for as the Hebrews had to overcome the original inhabitants of Canaan before they could enjoy their portion, so faith has to surmount many obstacles if it is to "possess its possessions." Nevertheless, that land of milk and honey into which Israel entered after the bondage of Egypt and the hardships of the wilderness were left behind, was manifestly a figure of the Christian's portion in heaven after he is forever done with sin in this world.

"Thou shalt call his name Jesus, for he shall save his people from their sins" (Matt. 1:21). First, save them from the pleasure or love of sin by bestowing a nature which hates it: this is the great *miracle* of grace. Second, save them from the penalty or punishment of sin, by remitting all its guilt: that is the grand *marvel* of grace. Third, save them from the power or dominion of sin, by the workings of His Spirit: this reveals the wondrous *might* of grace. Fourth, save them from the presence or inbeing of sin: this will demonstrate the glorious *magnitude* of grace. May it please the Lord to bless these elementary but most important thoughts to many of His little ones, and make their "big" brothers and sisters smaller in their own esteem.

PART FIVE
Heartwork

23 Introduction

"Do you think you came into this world to spend your whole time and strength in your employments, your trades, your pleasures, unto the satisfaction of the will of the flesh and of the mind? Have you time enough to eat, to drink, to sleep, and talk unprofitably—it may be corruptly—in all sorts of unnecessary societies, but have not enough time to live unto God, in the very essentials of that life? Alas, you came into the world under this law: 'It is appointed unto men once to die, but after this the judgment' (Heb. 9:27), and the end (purpose) why your life is here granted unto you is that you may be prepared for that judgment. If this be neglected, if the principal part of your time be not improved with respect unto this end, you will yet fall under the sentence of it unto eternity" (John Owen, 1670).

Multitudes seem to be running, but few "pressing toward the mark"; many talk about salvation, but few experience the joy of it. There is much of the form of godliness, but little of the power of it. Oh, how rare it is to find any who know anything experientially of the power that separates from the world, delivers from self, defends from Satan, makes sin to be hated, Christ to be loved, Truth to be prized, and error and evil to be departed from. Where shall we find those who are denying self, taking up their cross daily, and following Christ in the path of obedience? Where are they who hail reproach, welcome shame, and endure persecution? Where are they who are truly getting prayer answered daily, on whose behalf God is showing Himself strong? Something is radically wrong somewhere. Yes, and as surely as the beating of the pulse is an index to the state of our most vital physical organ, so the lives of professing Christians make it unmistakably evident that their hearts are diseased!

"The eyes of the Lord run to and fro throughout the whole earth, to show himself strong in the behalf of them whose heart is perfect toward him" (II Chron. 16:9). Ah, do not the opening words indicate that those with "perfect" hearts are few and far between, that they are hard to locate? Surely, it does; and it has ever been the case. David cried, "Help, Lord; for the godly man ceaseth; for the faithful fail from among the children of men" (Ps. 12:1). The Lord Jesus had to lament, "I have labored in vain, I have spent my strength for nought" (Isa. 49:4). The apostle Paul declared, "I have no man likeminded, who will naturally care for your state. For all seek their own, not the things which are Jesus Christ's" (Phil. 2:20-21); "All they which are in Asia be turned away from me" (II Tim. 1:15). And things are neither better nor worse today. But, my reader, instead of talking about the "apostasy of Christendom," instead of being occupied with the empty profession all around us, what about your own hearts? Is *your* heart "perfect"? If so, even in these so-called "hard times," God is "showing himself strong" in your behalf; that is, He is working miracles for you, and ministering to you in a way that He is not to the empty professors. But if God is not so doing, then *your* heart is *not* "perfect" toward Him, and it is high time for you to take stock and get down to serious soul business.

24 What It Means to Keep the Heart

"Keep thy heart with all diligence; for out of it are the issues of life" (Prov. 4:23). The pains which multitudes have taken in religion are but lost labor. Like the Pharisees of old, they have been tithing anise and mint and cummin, but neglecting the weightier matters. Many have a zeal, but it is not according to knowledge; they are active, but their energies are misdirected; they have wrought "many wonderful works," but they are rejected of God. Why? Because their employments are self-selected or man-appointed, while the one great task which God has assigned is left unattended to. All outward actions are worthless while our hearts be not right with God. He will not so much as hear our prayers while we regard iniquity in our hearts (Ps. 66:18)! Let us, then, endeavor to point out what is signified by this supremely important exhortation.

To "keep" the heart signifies *to have the conscience exercised about all things.* In a number of passages "heart" and "conscience" signify one and the same thing (I Sam. 24:5; II Sam. 24:10; I John 3:21, etc.). The apostle Paul declared, "Herein do I exercise myself, to have always a conscience void of offence toward God, and toward men" (Acts 24:16), and herein he sets before us an example which we need to emulate. After the most careful and diligent manner we must strive to keep the conscience free from all offense in the discharge of every duty that God requires, and in rendering to every man what is due him. Though this is never perfectly attained in this life, every regenerate soul has a real concern for such a state of conscience. "A good conscience, in all things willing to live honestly" (Heb. 13:18) is worth far more than rubies.

This is to be something more than an empty wish which gets us nowhere. The apostle said, "Herein do I *exercise* myself": it was a matter of deep concern to him, and one to which he assiduously applied himself. He labored hard in seeing to it that his conscience did not flatter, deceiving and misleading him. He was conscientious over both his outer and inner life, so that his conscience accused and condemned him not. He was more careful not to offend his conscience than he was to displease his dearest friend. He made it his daily business to live by this rule, abstaining from many a thing into which natural inclination drew him, and performing many a duty which the ease-loving flesh would shirk. He steadily maintained a care not to break the law of love toward either God or man. And, when conscious of failure, he saw to it that by renewed acts of repentance and faith (in confession) each offense was removed from his conscience, instead of allowing guilt to accumulate thereon.

"Now the end of the commandment is charity [love] out of a pure heart, and of a good conscience, and of faith unfeigned" (I Tim. 1:5). The "commandment" is the same as the "holy commandment" of II Peter 2:21, namely the gospel, as including the moral law, which enjoined perfect love both to God and to our neighbor. The "end" or design—that which is enjoined and whose accomplishment is prompted thereby—is *love.* But spiritual "love" can proceed only from "a pure heart," that is one which has been renewed by grace, and thereby delivered from enmity against God (Rom. 8:7) and hatred against man (Titus 3:3), and cleansed from the love and pollution of sin. Spiritual "love" can proceed only out of a "good conscience," that is a conscience which has been made tender and active by grace, which has been purged by the blood of Christ, and which sedulously avoids all that defiles it and draws away from God; its possessor being influenced to act conscientiously in the whole of his conduct. It is solemn to note that those who "put away" a good conscience soon make "shipwreck of the faith" (I Tim. 1:19).

To "keep" the heart means to *"set the Lord alway before"* us (Ps. 16:8). Some may object that those words spoke, prophetically, of the Lord Jesus. True, but remember He has "left us an example *that we should follow* his steps." What, then, is it to "set the Lord alway before" us? It means to remember that we must render to Him a full account of our stewardship, and to let this fact constantly influence us. It means that we are ever to have *His* honor and glory in view, living not to please ourselves but acting according to His revealed will. It means that we should strive, especially, to have *God* before our souls whenever we engage in any religious exercises. The Omniscient One will not be imposed upon by outward forms or empty words; they who worship Him "must worship him in spirit and in truth" (John 4:24). "Seek ye my face." Oh, to respond with David, "My *heart* said unto thee, thy face, Lord, will I seek" (Ps. 27:8).

"The well is seldom so full that water will at first pumping flow forth; neither is the heart commonly so spiritual—even after our best care in our worldly converse—as to pour itself into God's bosom freely, without something to raise and elevate it; yea, often the springs of grace lie so low, that pumping only will not fetch the heart up to a praying frame, but arguments must be poured into the soul before the affections rise" (W. Gurnall, 1660). Does not this explain why, after saying, "Bless the Lord, O my soul; and all that is within me, bless his holy name," the psalmist *added,* "Bless the Lord, O my soul" (Ps. 103:1-2)?

Ah, note well those words, dear reader: "Bless the Lord, O my *soul,*" and not merely by the lips. David dreaded lest, while the outward was awake, his inner man should be asleep. Are you equally careful as to this? David labored so that no dullness and drowsiness should steal over his faculties. Therefore did he add, "*And all that is within me,* bless his holy name"—understanding, conscience, affections, and will. Oh, that we may not be guilty of that awful sin about which Christ complained, "This people draweth nigh unto me with their mouth; *but their heart is far from me*" (Matt. 15:8). Again we would note the repetition in verse 2, "Bless the Lord, *O my soul*": how this shows us that we need to bestir ourselves repeatedly when about to approach the Majesty on high, seeking with all our might to throw off the spirit of sloth, formality, and hypocrisy.

Of old God's servant complained, "There is none that calleth upon thy name, that *stirreth up himself* to take hold of thee" (Isa. 64:7). Are we any better, my friends? Do *we* really bestir ourselves to "take hold" of God? We shall never be like Jacob—successful "wrestlers" with Him—until we do. There is little wonder that so few obtain answers to their petitions unto the throne of grace: it is not simply prayer, but "the effectual *fervent* prayer of a righteous man that availeth much" (James 5:16). Before seeking to approach the Most High we need to "prepare" our heart (Job 11:13), and beg God to "strengthen" it (Ps. 27:14), so that we may trust in Him with all our hearts (Prov. 3:6), love Him with all our hearts (Matt. 22:37), and praise Him with the whole heart (Ps. 9:1).

Oh, the frightful impiety which is now to be witnessed on almost every side, of heedlessly rushing into the holy presence of God (or rather going through the form of doing so), and gabbling off the first things that come to mind. And all of us are more affected by this evil spirit than we imagine, for "evil communications corrupt good manners" (I Cor. 15:33). We need definitely to seek grace and fight against so grievously insulting God. We need to fix our minds steadily on the august perfections of God, reminding ourselves of *who* it is we are about to approach. We need to seek deliverance from that half-hearted, ill-conceived, careless, and indifferent worship which is offered by so many. We need to ponder God's grace and goodness unto us, and lay hold of His encouraging promises, that our affections may be inflamed and our souls brought into that gracious temper which is suited unto Him to whom we owe our all.

But we need diligently to watch our hearts not only when about to approach God in prayer or worship, but also when turning to His holy Word. All ordinances, helps, and means of grace are but empty shells unless we meet with God in them, and for that He must be sought: "Ye shall seek me, and find me, when ye shall search for me with all your heart" (Jer. 29:13). We are not at all likely to obtain anymore soul profit from the reading of the Scriptures than we are from the perusal of men's writings if we approach them in the same spirit as we do human books. God's Word is addressed unto the conscience, and it is only as we strive to have our hearts suitably affected by what we read therein that we may justly expect to be helped spiritually.

God has bidden us, "My son, keep thy father's commandment, and forsake not the law of thy mother: bind them continually upon thine heart" (Prov. 6:20-21). And again, "Keep my commandments, and live: and my law as the apple of thine eye. Bind them upon thy fingers, write them upon the table of thine heart" (Prov. 7:2-3). This cannot be done by reading the Bible for a few minutes, and then an hour later forgetting what has been read. Shame on us that we should treat God's Word so lightly. No, we must "meditate" therein day and night" (Ps. 1:2). Unless we do so, we shall never be able to say, "Thy word have I hid in mine heart, that I might not sin against thee" (Ps. 119:11); nor shall we be able to say, "I have inclined my heart to perform thy statutes alway" (Ps. 119:112).

To "keep" the heart signifies *attending diligently to its progress or decay in holiness.* What health is to the body holiness is to the soul. "I commune with mine own heart: and my spirit made diligent search" (Ps. 77:6). This is absolutely essential if a healthy spiritual life is to be maintained; a part of each day should be set aside for the study of the heart and the cultivation of its faculties. The more this is done, the less difficulty shall we experience in knowing what to pray for! Shame on us that we are so diligent in thinking about and caring for our bodies, while the state of our souls is so rarely inquired after. Emulate the example of Hezekiah, who "humbled himself for the pride of his heart" (II Chron. 32:26). Peter's heart was lifted up with self-confidence: his fall was preceded by "a haughty spirit."

It is *in the heart* that all backsliding begins. Observe closely your affections, and see whether God or the world is gaining ground in them. Watch whether you experience increasing profit and pleasure in reading God's Word, or whether you have to force yourself to it in order to discharge a duty. Observe the same thing in connection with prayer: whether you are finding increased or decreased liberty in pouring out your heart to God; whether you are having more freedom in so doing, or whether it is becoming an irksome task. Examine well your spiritual graces, and ascertain whether your faith be in lively exercise, feeding upon the precepts and promises of God; whether your hope is lively, anticipating the glorious future; whether your love be fervent or cold; whether patience, meekness, self-control be greater or less.

To "keep" the heart signifies *to store it well with pure and holy things.* As the most effective way of getting a child willingly to drop some dirty trifle is to proffer it an apple or orange, so the best security for the soul against the allurements of Satan is to have it engaged with a lovelier and more satisfying object. A heart which is filled and engaged with good is best protected against evil. Note well the order in Philippians 4:6, 8. "Be anxious for nothing; but in every thing by prayer and supplication with thanksgiving let your requests be made known unto God. And the peace of God, which passeth all understanding, shall keep your hearts and minds through Christ Jesus. Finally, brethren, whatsoever things are true, whatsoever things are honest, whatsoever things are just, whatsoever things are pure, whatsoever things are lovely, whatsoever things are of good report; if there be any virtue, and if there be any praise, *think on these things.*" The heart which casts all its care upon God is well guarded from anxiety by His peace; but a pure atmosphere must be breathed if the soul is to be kept healthy, and that is best promoted by thinking about wholesome, lovely, and praise-provoking things.

Commune frequently with Christ: dwell upon His loveliness, stay in the sunshine of His presence, refresh your soul with those gifts and graces He is ever ready to bestow, and you shall have in yourself "a well of water springing up into everlasting life" (John 4:14). "Were our affections filled, taken up, and possessed with these things [the beauty of God and the glory of Christ], as it is our duty that they should be, and as it is our happiness when they are, what access could sin—with its painted pleasures, with its sugared poisons, with its envenomed baits—have upon our souls? How we should loathe all its proposals, and say unto them, 'Get you hence as an abominable thing' " (John Owen).

As well might a poor man expect to be rich in this world without industry, or a weak man to become strong and healthy without food and exercise, as a Christian to be rich in faith and strong in the Lord without earnest endeavor and diligent effort. It is true that all our labors amount to nothing unless the Lord blesses them (Ps. 127:1), as it also is that apart from Him we can do nothing (John 15:5). Nevertheless, God places no premium upon sloth, and has promised that "the soul of the diligent shall be made fat" (Prov. 13:4). A farmer may be fully persuaded of his own helplessness to make his fields productive, he may realize that their fertility is dependent upon the sovereign will of God, and he may also be a firm believer in the efficacy of prayer; but unless he discharges *his own duty his barns will be empty.* So it is spiritually.

God has not called His people to be drones, nor to maintain an attitude of passiveness. No, He bids them work, toil, labor. The sad thing is that so many of them are engaged in the wrong task, or, at least, giving more of their attention to that which is incidental, and neglecting that which is essential and fundamental. "Keep thy heart with all diligence" (Prov. 4:23): *this* is the great task which God has assigned unto each of His children. But oh, how sadly is the heart neglected! Of all their concerns and possessions, the *least* diligence is used by the vast majority of professing Christians in the keeping of their hearts. As long as they safeguard their other interests—their reputations, their bodies, their positions in the world—the heart may be left to take its own course.

As the heart in our physical body is the center and fountain of life, because from it blood circulates into every part, conveying with it either health or disease, so it is with us spiritually. If our heart be the residence of impiety, pride, avarice, malice, impure lusts, then the whole current of our lives will largely be tainted with these vices. If they are admitted there and prevail for a season, then our character and conduct will be proportionately affected. Therefore, the citadel of the heart needs above all things to be well guarded, that it may not be seized by those numerous and watchful assailants which are ever attacking it. This spring needs to be well protected that its waters be not poisoned.

The man is what his heart is. If *this* be dead to God, then nothing in him is alive. If *this* be right with God, all will be right. As the mainspring of a watch sets all its wheels and parts in motion, so as a man "thinketh in his heart, so is he" (Prov. 23:7). If the heart be right, the actions will be. As a man's heart is, such is his state now and will be hereafter: if it be regenerated and sanctified there will be a life of faith and holiness in this world, and everlasting life will be enjoyed in the world to come. Therefore, "rather look to the cleansing of thine heart, than to the cleansing of thy well; rather look to the feeding of thine heart, than to the feeding of thy flock; rather look to the defending of thine heart, than to the defending of thine house; rather look to the keeping of thine heart, than to the keeping of thy money" (Peter Moffat, 1570).

"Keep thy heart with all diligence, for out of it are the issues of life" (Prov. 4:23). The "heart" is here put for our whole inner being, the "hidden man of the heart" (I Peter 3:4). It is that which controls and gives character to all that we do. To "keep"—garrison or guard—the heart or soul is the great work which God has assigned us: the enablement is His, but the duty is ours. We are to keep the imagination from vanity, the understanding from error, the will from perverseness, the conscience clear of guilt, the affections from being inordinate and set on evil objects, the mind from being employed on worthless or vile subjects; the whole from being possessed by Satan. This is the work to which God has called us.

Rightly did the Puritan John Favel say, "The keeping and right managing of the heart in every condition is the great business of a Christian's life." Now to "keep" the heart right implies that it has been *set right*. Thus it was at regeneration, when it was given a new spiritual bent. True conversion is the heart turning from Satan's control to God's, from sin to holiness, from the world to Christ. To *keep* the heart right signifies the constant care and diligence of the renewed person to preserve his soul in that holy frame to which grace has reduced it and daily strives to hold it. "Hereupon do all events depend: the heart being kept, the whole course of our life here will be according to the mind of God, and the end of it will be the enjoyment of Him hereafter. This being neglected, life will be lost, both here as unto obedience, and hereafter as to glory" (John Owen in *Causes of Apostasy*).

A. *To "keep" the heart means striving to shut out from it all that is opposed to God.* "Little children, keep yourselves from idols" (I John 5:21). God is a jealous God and will brook no rival; He claims the throne of our hearts, and requires that we love Him supremely. When we perceive our affections being inordinately drawn out unto any earthly object, we are to fight against it, and "resist the devil." When Paul said, "All things are lawful unto me, but all things are not expedient: all things are lawful for me, but I will not be *brought under the power* of any" (I Cor. 6:12), he signified that he was keeping his heart diligently, that he was jealous lest *things* should gain that esteem and place in his soul which was due alone unto the Lord. A very small object placed immediately before the eye is sufficient to shut out the light of the sun, and trifling things taken up by the affections may soon sever communion with the Holy One.

Before regeneration our hearts were deceitful above all things, and desperately wicked (Jer. 17:9): that was because the evil principle, the "flesh," had complete dominion over them. But inasmuch as "the flesh" remains in us after conversion, and is constantly striving for the mastery over "the spirit," the Christian needs to exercise a constant watchful jealousy over his heart, mindful of its readiness to be imposed upon, and its proneness unto a compliance with temptations. All the avenues to the heart need to be carefully guarded so that nothing hurtful enters therein, particularly against vain thoughts and imaginations, and especially in those seasons when they are apt to gain an advantage. For if injurious thoughts are suffered to gain an inroad into the mind, if we accustom ourselves to give them entertainment, then in vain shall we hope to be "spiritually minded" (Rom. 8:6). All such thoughts are only making provision to fulfill the lusts of the flesh.

Thus, for the Christian to "keep" his heart with all diligence means for him to pay close attention to the direction in which his affections are moving, to discover whether the things of the world are gaining a firmer and fuller hold over him or whether they are increasingly losing their charm for him. God has exhorted us, "Set your affections on things above, not on things on the earth" (Col. 3:2), and the heeding of this injunction calls for constant examination of the heart to discover whether or not it is becoming more and more dead unto this deceitful and perishing world, and whether heavenly things are those in which we find our chief and greatest delight. "Take heed to thyself, and keep thy soul diligently, lest thou forget the things which thine eyes have seen, and lest they depart from thy heart" (Deut. 4:9).

B. *To "keep" the heart means striving to bring it into conformity with the Word.* We are not to rest content until an actual image of its pure and holy teachings is stamped upon it. Alas, so many today are just *playing* with the solemn realities of God, allowing them to flit across their fancy, but never embracing and making them their own. Why is it, dear reader, that those solemn impressions you had when hearing a searching sermon or reading a searching article so quickly faded away? Why did not those holy feelings and aspirations which were stirred within you last? Why have they borne no fruit? Was it not because you failed to see that your heart was duly affected by them? You failed to "hold fast" that which you had "received and heard" (Rev. 3:3), and in consequence your heart became absorbed again in "the care of this life" or "the deceitfulness of riches," and thus the Word was choked.

It is not enough to hear or read a powerful message from one of God's servants, and to be deeply interested and stirred by it. If there be no diligent effort on your part, then it will be said that "your goodness is as a morning cloud, and as the early dew it goeth away" (Hos. 6:4). What, then, is required? This: earnest and persevering prayer that God will fasten the message in your soul as a nail in a sure place, so that the devil himself cannot catch it away. What is required? This: "Mary kept all these things, and pondered them in her heart" (Luke 2:19). Things which are not duly pondered are soon forgotten: meditation stands to reading as mastication does to eating. What is required? This: that you promptly put into practice what you have learned; walk according to the light God has given, or it will quickly be taken from you (Luke 8:18).

Not only must the outward actions be regulated by the Word, but the heart must also be conformed thereto. It is not enough to abstain from murder, the causeless anger must be put away. It is not enough to abstain from the act of adultery, the inward lust must be mortified, too (Matt. 5:28). God not only takes note of and keeps a record of all our external conduct, but He "weigheth the spirits" (Prov. 16:2). Not only so. He requires *us* to scrutinize the springs from which our actions proceed, to examine our motives, to ponder *the spirit* in which we act. God requires truth—that is sincerity, reality—in "the inward parts" (Ps. 51:6). Therefore does He command us. "Keep thy heart with all diligence, for out of it are the issues of life."

C. *To "keep" the heart means to preserve it tender unto sin.* The unregenerate man makes little or no distinction between sin and crime; as long as he keeps within the law of the land, and maintains a reputation for respectability among his fellows, he is, generally speaking, quite satisfied with himself. But it is far otherwise with one who has been born again: he has been awakened to the fact that he has to do with *God,* and must yet render a full account unto Him. He makes conscience of a hundred things which the unconverted never trouble themselves about. When the Holy Spirit first convicted him he was made to feel that his whole life had been one of rebellion against God, of pleasing himself. The consciousness of this pierced him to the quick: his inward anguish far exceeded any pains of body or sorrow occasioned by temporal losses. He saw himself to be a spiritual leper, and hated himself for it, and mourned bitterly before God. He cried, "Hide thy face from my sins, and blot out all mine iniquities. Create in me a clean heart, O God; and renew a right spirit within me" (Ps. 51:9-10).

Now, it is the duty of the Christian, and part of the task which God has set him, to see to it that this sense of the exceeding sinfulness of sin be not lost. He is to labor daily that his heart be duly affected by the heinousness of self-will and self-love. He is steadfastly to resist every effort of Satan to make him pity himself, think lightly of wrongdoing, or excuse himself in the same. He is to live in the constant realization that the eye of God is ever upon him, so that when tempted he will say with Joseph, "How then can I do this great wickedness, and sin against God?" (Gen. 39:9). He is to view sin in the light of the cross, daily reminding himself that it was *his* iniquities which caused the Lord of glory to be made a curse for him; employing the dying love of Christ as a motive why he must not allow himself in anything that is contrary to the holiness and obedience which the Saviour asks from all His redeemed.

Ah, my Christian reader, it is no child's play to "keep the heart with all diligence." The easy-going religion of our day will never take its devotees (or rather its *victims!*) to heaven. The question has been asked, "Who shall ascend into the hill of the Lord? or *who* shall stand in his holy place?" and plainly has the question been answered by God Himself: "He that hath clean hands, and a pure heart . . . " (Ps. 24:3-4). Equally plain is the teaching of the New Testament, "Blessed are the pure in heart: for *they* shall see God" (Matt. 5:8). A "pure heart" is one that hates sin, which makes conscience of sin, which grieves over it, which strives against it. A "pure heart" is one that seeks to keep undefiled the temple of the Holy Spirit, the dwelling place of Christ (Eph. 3:17).

D. *To "keep" the heart means to look diligently after its cleansing.* Perhaps some of our readers often find themselves sorrowfully crying, "Oh, the vileness of my heart!" Thank God if He *has* discovered this to you; if such be so, and you really feel it, it is clear proof that He has made you to differ from the multitudes of blindly indifferent professing Christians all around you. But, dear friend, there is no sufficient reason why your "heart" should *continue* to be vile. You might lament that your garden was overgrown with weeds and filled with rubbish; but need it remain so? We speak not now of your sinful *nature,* the incurable and unchangeable "flesh" which still indwells you; but of your *"heart,"* which God bids you "keep." You *are* responsible to purge your mind of vain imaginations, your soul of unlawful affections, your conscience of guilt.

But, alas, you say, "I have no control over such things: they come unbidden and I am powerless to prevent them." So the devil would have you believe! Revert again to the analogy of your garden. Do not the weeds spring up unbidden? Do not the slugs and other pests seek to prey upon the plants? What then? Do you merely bewail your helplessness? No, you resist them, and take means to keep them under. Thieves enter houses uninvited, but whose fault is it if the doors and windows be left unfastened? Oh, heed not the seductive lullabies of Satan. God says, "Purify your hearts, ye double minded" (James 4:8); that is, one mind for Him, and another for self! one for holiness, and another for the pleasures of sin.

But *how* am I to "purify" my heart? By vomiting up the foul things taken into it, shamefacedly owning them before God, repudiating them, turning from them with loathing; and it is written, "If we confess our sins, he is faithful and just to forgive us our sins, and to *cleanse* us from all unrighteousness." By daily renewing our exercise of repentance, and *such* repentance as is spoken of in II Corinthians 7:11: "For behold this self-same thing, that ye sorrowed after a godly sort, what carefulness it wrought in you, yea, what clearing of yourselves, yea, what indignation, yea, what fear, yea, what vehement desire, yea, what zeal, yea, what revenge! In all things ye have approved yourselves to be clear in this matter." By the daily exercise of faith (Acts 15:9), appropriating afresh the cleansing blood of Christ, bathing every night in that "fountain" which has been opened "for sin and uncleanness" (Zech. 13:1). By treading the path of God's commandments: "Seeing ye have purified your souls in obeying the truth through the Spirit" (I Peter 1:22).

We close by pointing out what is obvious to every Christian reader, namely that such a task calls for divine aid. Help and grace need to be earnestly and definitely sought of the Holy Spirit each day. We should bow before God, and in all simplicity say, "Lord, Thou requirest me to keep my heart with all diligence, and I feel utterly incompetent for such a task; such a work lies altogether beyond my poor feeble powers; therefore I humbly ask Thee in the name of Christ graciously to grant unto me supernatural strength to do as Thou hast bidden me. Lord, work in me both to will and to do of Thy good pleasure."

25 How Shall We Labor to Keep the Heart?

"Man looketh on the outward appearance, but the Lord looketh on the heart" (I Sam. 16:7). How prone we are to be occupied with that which is evanescent, rather than with the things that abide; how ready to gauge things by our senses instead of by our rational powers. How easily we are deceived by that which is on the surface, forgetting that true beauty lies within. How slow we are to adopt God's way of estimating. Instead of being attracted by comeliness of physical features we should value moral qualities and spiritual graces. Instead of spending so much care, time, and money on the adorning of the body we ought to devote our best attention to the developing and directing of the faculties of our souls. Alas, the vast majority of our fellows live as though they had no souls, and the average professing Christian gives little serious thought to the same.

Yes, the Lord "looketh on the heart": He sees its thoughts and intents, knows its desires and designs, beholds its motives and motions, and deals with us accordingly. The Lord discerns what qualities are in our hearts: what holiness and righteousness, what wisdom and prudence, what justice and integrity, what mercy and kindness. When such graces are lively and flourishing, then is fulfilled that verse, "My beloved is gone down into his garden, to the beds of spices, to feed in the gardens, and to gather lilies" (Song of Sol. 6:2). God esteems nothing so highly as holy faith, unfeigned love, and filial fear; in His sight a "meek and quiet spirit" is of "great price" (I Peter 3:4).

The sincerity of our profession largely depends upon the care and conscience we have in keeping our hearts. A very searching example of this is found in II Kings 10:31, "But Jehu took no heed to walk in the law of the Lord God of Israel with all his heart." Those words are more solemn because of what is said of him in the previous verse: "And the Lord said unto Jehu, Because thou hast done well in executing that which is right in mine eyes, and hast done unto the house of Ahab according unto all that was in mine heart, thy children of the fourth generation shall sit on the throne of Israel." Jehu was partial in his reformation, which showed his heart was not right with God; he abhorred the worship of Baal which Ahab had fostered, but he tolerated the golden calves which Jeroboam had set up. He failed to put away all the evil.

Ah, my reader, true conversion is not only turning away from gross sin, it is the heart forsaking *all* sin. There must be no reserve, for God will not allow any idol, nor must we. Jehu went so far, but he stopped short of the vital point; he put away evil, but he did not do that which was good. He heeded not the law of the Lord to walk in it *"with all his heart."* It is greatly to be feared that those who are heedless are graceless, for where the principle of holiness is planted in the heart it makes its possessor circumspect and desirous of pleasing God in all things—not from servile fear, but from grateful love; not by constraint, but freely; not occasionally, but constantly.

"Keep thine heart with all diligence." Guard it jealously as the dwelling place of Him to whom you have given it. Guard it with the utmost vigilance, for not only is there the enemy without seeking entrance, but there is a traitor within desirous of dominion. The Hebrew for "with all diligence" literally rendered is "above all"; above all the concerns of our outward life, for, careful as we should be as to that, it is before the eyes of men, whereas the heart is the object of *God's* holy gaze. Then "keep" or preserve it more sedulously than your reputation, your body, your estate, your money. With all earnestness and prayer, labor that no evil desire prevails or abides there, avoiding all that excites lust, feeds pride, or stirs up anger, crushing the first emotions of such evils as you would the brood of a scorpion.

Many people place great expectations in varied circumstances and conditions. One thinks he could serve God much better if he were more prospered temporally; another if he passed through the refining effects of poverty and affliction. One thinks his spirituality would be promoted if he could be more retired and solitary; another if only he could have more society and Christian fellowship. But, my reader, the only way to serve God better is to be content with the place in which He has put you, and therein *get a better heart!* We shall never enter into the advantages of any situation, nor overcome the disadvantages of any condition, until we fix and water the root of them in ourselves. "Make the tree good, *and* his fruit good" (Matt. 12:33): get the heart right, and you will soon be superior unto all "circumstances."

"But how can I get my heart right? Can the Ethiopian change his skin or the leopard his spots?" Answer: You are creating your own difficulty by confounding "heart" with "nature"; they are quite distinct. It is important to recognize this, for many are confused thereon. There has been such an undue emphasis upon the "two natures in the Christian" that often it has been lost sight of that the Christian is *a person* over and above his two natures. The Scriptures make the distinction clear enough. For example, God does not bid us keep our "nature," but He does our "hearts." We do not believe with our "nature," but we do with our "hearts" (Rom. 10:10). God never tells us to "rend" our nature (Joel 2:13), "circumcise" our nature (Deut. 10:6) or "purify" our nature (James 4:8), but He does our "hearts"! The "heart" is the very center of our responsibility, and to deny that we are to improve and keep it is to repudiate human accountability.

It is the devil who seeks to persuade people that they are not responsible for the state of their hearts, and may no more change them than they can the stars in their courses. And the "flesh" within finds such a lie very agreeable to its case. But he who has been regenerated by the sovereign grace of God cannot, with the Scriptures before him, give heed unto any such delusion. While he has to deplore how sadly neglected is the great task which God has set before him, while he has to bemoan his wretched failure to make his heart what it ought to be, nevertheless he wants to do better; and after his duty has been pressed upon him he will daily seek grace better to discharge his duty, and instead of being totally discouraged by the difficulty and greatness of the work required he will cry the more fervently to the Holy Spirit for His enablement.

The Christian who means business will labor to have a "willing" heart (Exod. 35:5), which acts spontaneously and gladly, not of necessity; a "perfect" heart (I Chron. 29:9), sincere, genuine, upright; a "tender" heart (II Chron. 34:26), yielding and pliable, the opposite of hard and stubborn; a "broken" heart (Ps. 34:18), sorrowing over all failure and sin; a "united" heart (Ps. 86:11), all the affections centered on God; an "enlarged" heart (Ps. 119:32), delighting in *every* part of Scripture and loving all God's people; a "sound" heart (Prov. 14:30), right in doctrine and practice; a "merry" heart (Prov. 15:15), rejoicing in the Lord alway; a "pure" heart (Matt. 5:8), hating all evil; an "honest and good heart" (Luke 8:15), free from guile and hypocrisy, willing to be searched through and through by the Word; a "single" heart (Eph. 6:5), desiring only God's glory; a "true" heart (Heb. 10:22), genuine in all its dealings with God.

The duty of keeping the heart with the utmost diligence is binding upon the Christian at all times; there is no period or condition of life in which he may be excused from this work. Nevertheless, there are distinctive seasons, critical hours, which call for more than a common vigilance over the heart, and it is a few of these which we would now contemplate, seeking help from above to point out some of the most effectual aids unto the right accomplishment of the task God has assigned us. General principles are always needful and beneficial, yet details have to be furnished if we are to know how to apply them in particular circumstances. It is this lack of definiteness which constitutes one of the most glaring defects in so much modern ministry.

A. *In times of prosperity.* When providence smiles upon us and bestows temporal gifts with a lavish hand, then has the Christian urgent reason to keep his heart with all diligence, for that is the time we are apt to grow careless, proud, earthly. Therefore was Israel cautioned of old, "And it shall be, when the Lord thy God shall have brought thee into the land which he sware unto thy fathers, to Abraham, to Isaac, and to Jacob, to give thee great and goodly cities, which thou buildedst not, and houses full of good things, which thou filledst not, and wells digged, which thou diggedst not, vineyards and olive trees, which thou plantedst not; when thou shalt have eaten and be full; *then beware* lest thou forget the Lord" (Deut. 6:10-12). Alas that they heeded not that exhortation.

Many are the warnings furnished in Scripture. Of Uzziah it is recorded, "When he was strong, his heart was lifted up to his destruction" (II Chron. 26:16). To the king of Tyre, God said, "Thine heart is lifted up, because of thy riches" (Ezek. 28:5). Of Israel we read, "And they took strong cities, and a fat land, and possessed houses full of all goods, wells digged, vineyards and oliveyards, and fruit trees in abundance: so they did eat, and were filled, and became fat, and delighted themselves in thy great goodness. *Nevertheless* they were disobedient, and rebelled against thee, and cast thy law behind their backs, and slew thy prophets which testified against them to turn them to thee" (Neh. 9:25-26). And again, "Of their silver and their gold have they made them idols" (Hos. 8:4).

Sad indeed are the above passages, the more so because we have seen such a tragic repetition of them in our own days. Oh, the earthly mindedness which prevailed, the indulging of the flesh, the sinful extravagance, which were seen among professing Christians while "times were good"! How practical godliness waned, how the denying of self disappeared, how covetousness, pleasure, and wantonness possessed the great majority of those calling themselves the people of God. Yet great as was their sin, far greater was that of most of the preachers, who, instead of warning, admonishing, rebuking, and setting before their people an example of sobriety and thrift, criminally remained silent upon the crying sins of their hearers, and themselves encouraged the reckless spending of money and the indulgence of worldly lusts. How, then, is the Christian to keep his heart from these things in times of prosperity?

First, by seriously pondering the dangerous and ensnaring temptations which attend a prosperous condition, for very, very few of those who live in the prosperity and pleasures of this world escape eternal perdition. "It is easier [said Christ] for a camel to go through the eye of a needle, than for a rich man to enter into the kingdom of heaven" (Matt. 19:24). What multitudes have been carried to hell in the cushioned chariots of earthly wealth and ease, while a comparative handful have been shipped to heaven by the rod of affliction. Remember, too, that many of the Lord's own people have sadly deteriorated in seasons of worldly success. When Israel was in a low condition in the wilderness, then were they "holiness unto the Lord" (Jer. 2:3); but when fed in the fat pastures of Canaan they said, "We are lords; we will come no more unto thee" (v. 31).

Second, diligently seek grace to heed that word, "If riches increase, set not your heart upon them" (Ps. 62:10). Those riches may be given to try you; not only are they most uncertain things, often taking to themselves wings and flying swiftly away, but at best they cannot satisfy the soul, and only perish with the using. Remember that God values no man a jot more for these things: He esteems us by inward graces, and not by outward possessions: "In every nation he that feareth him, and worketh righteousness, is accepted with him" (Acts 10:35). Third, urge upon your soul the consideration of that awful day of reckoning, wherein according to our receipt of mercies so shall be our accountings of them: "For unto whomsoever much is given, of him shall be much required" (Luke 12:48). Each of us must yet give an account of our stewardship.

B. *In times of adversity.* When providence frowns upon us, overturning our cherished plans, and blasting our outward comforts, then has the Christian urgent need to look to his heart, and keep it with all diligence from replying against God or fainting under His hand. Job was a mirror of patience, yet his heart was discomposed by trouble. Jonah was a man of God, yet he was peevish under trial. When the food supplies gave out in the wilderness, they who had been miraculously delivered from Egypt and who sang Jehovah's praises so heartily at the Red Sea murmured and rebelled. It takes much grace to keep the heart calm amid the storms of life, to keep the spirit sweet when there is much to embitter the flesh, and to say, "The Lord gave, and the Lord hath taken away; blessed be the name of the Lord." Yet this is a Christian duty!

To help thereunto, first consider, fellow Christian, that despite these cross providences God is still faithfully carrying out the great design of electing love upon the souls of His people, and orders these very afflictions as means sanctified to that end. Nothing happens by chance, but all by divine counsel (Eph. 1:11) and, therefore, it is that "all things work together *for good* to them that love God, to them who are the called according to his purpose" (Rom. 8:28). Ah, beloved, it will wonderfully calm your troubled breast and sustain your fainting heart to rest upon that blessed fact. The poor worldling may say, "The bottom has dropped out of everything," but not so the saint, for the eternal God is *his* refuge, and underneath him are still the "everlasting arms."

It is ignorance or forgetfulness of God's loving designs which makes us so prone to chafe under His providential dealings. If faith were more in exercise we should "count it all joy" when we fall into divers temptations, or trials (James 1:2). Why so? Because we should discern that those very trials were sent to wean our hearts from this empty world, to tear down pride and carnal security, to refine us. If, then, my Father has a design of love unto my soul, do I well to be angry with Him? Later, if not now, you will see that those bitter disappointments were blessings in disguise, and will exclaim, "It is good for me that I have been afflicted" (Ps. 119:71).

26 The Importance of Keeping the Heart

"God is not the author of confusion" (I Cor. 14:33); no, the devil causes that, and he has succeeded in creating much in the thinking of many, by confounding the "heart" with the "nature." People say, "I was born with an evil heart, and I cannot help it." It would be more correct to say, "I was born with an evil nature, which I am responsible to subdue." The Christian needs clearly to recognize that *in addition to* his two "natures"—the flesh and the spirit—he has a heart which God requires him to "keep." We have already touched upon this point, but deem it advisable to add a further word thereon. I cannot change or better my "nature," but I may and must my "heart." For example, "nature" is slothful and loves ease, but the Christian is to redeem the time and be zealous of good works. Nature hates the thought of death, but the Christian should bring his heart to desire to depart and be with Christ.

The popular religion of the day is either a head or a hand one: that is to say, the laboring to acquire a larger and fuller intellectual group of the things of God or a constant round of activities called "service for the Lord." But the *heart* is neglected! Thousands are reading, studying, taking "Bible courses," but for all the *spiritual* benefits their souls derive they might as well be engaged in breaking stones. Lest it be thought that such a stricture is too severe, we quote a sentence from a letter recently received from one who has completed no less than eight of these "Bible study courses": "There was nothing in that 'hard work' which ever called for self-examination, which led me really to know God, and appropriate the Scriptures to my deep need." No, of course there was not: their compilers—like nearly all the speakers at the big "Bible conferences"—studiously avoid all that is unpalatable to the flesh, all that condemns the natural man, all that pierces and searches the conscience. Oh, the tragedy of this *head* "Christianity."

Equally pitiable is the *hand* religion of the day, when young "converts" are put to teaching a Sunday school class, urged to "speak" in the open air, or take up "personal work." How many thousands of beardless youths and young girls are now engaged in what is called "winning souls for Christ," when *their own* souls are spiritually starved! They may "memorize" two or three verses of Scripture a day, but that does not mean their souls are being fed. How many are giving their evenings to helping in some "mission," when they need to be spending the time in "the secret place of the Most High"! And how many bewildered souls are using the major part of the Lord's Day in rushing from one meeting to another instead of seeking from God that which will fortify them against the temptations of the week! Oh, the tragedy of this *hand* "Christianity."

How subtle the devil is! Under the guise of promoting growth in "the knowledge of the Lord," he gets people to attend a ceaseless round of meetings, or to read an almost endless number of religious periodicals and books; or under the pretense of "honoring the Lord" by all this so-called "service" he induces the one or the other to *neglect* the great task which *God* has set before us: "keep thy heart with all diligence; for out of it are the issues of life" (Prov. 4:23). Ah, it is far easier to speak to others than it is constantly to use and improve all holy means and duties to preserve the soul from sin, and maintain it in sweet and free communion with God. It is far easier to spend an hour reading a sensational article upon "the signs of the times" than it is to spend an hour in agonizing before God for purifying and rectifying grace!

This work of keeping the heart is *of supreme importance.* The total disregard of it means that we are mere formalists. "My son, give me thine heart" (Prov. 23:26): until *that* be done, God will accept nothing from us. The prayers and praises of our lips, the labor of our hands, yea, and a correct outward walk, are things of no value in *His* sight while the heart be estranged from Him. As the inspired apostle declared, "Though I speak with the tongues of men and of angels, and have not *love,* I am become as sounding brass, or a tinkling cymbal. And though I have the gift of prophecy, and understand all mysteries, and all knowledge; and though I have all faith, so that I could remove mountains, and have not *love,* I am nothing: And though I bestow all my goods to feed the poor, and though I give my body to be burned, and have not *love,* it profiteth nothing" (I Cor. 13:1-3). If the heart be not right with God, we cannot *worship* Him, though we may go through the form of it. Watch diligently, then, your love for *Him.*

God cannot be imposed upon, and he who takes *no* care to order his heart aright before Him is a hypocrite. "And they come unto thee as the people cometh, and they sit before thee as my people, and they hear thy words, but they will not do them; for with their mouth they show much love, *but their heart* goeth after their covetousness. And, lo, thou art unto them as a very lovely song of one that hath a pleasant voice, and can play well on an instrument" (Ezek. 33:31-32). Here are a company of formal hypocrites, as is evident from the words "*as* my people": *like* them, but *not of* them. And what constituted them impostors? Their outside was very fair—high professions, reverent postures, much seeming delight in the means of grace. Ah, but their *hearts* were not set on God, but, commanded by their lusts, went after covetousness.

But lest a real Christian should infer from the above that he is a hypocrite too, because many times his heart wanders, and he finds—strive all he may—that he cannot keep his mind stayed upon God when praying, reading His Word, or engaging in public worship, to him we answer that the objection carries its own refutation. You say, " . . . strive all I may"; ah, if you *have*, then the blessing of the upright is yours, even though God sees well to exercise you over the affliction of a wandering mind. There remains still much in the understanding and affections to humble you, but if you are *exercised* over them, strive against them, and *sorrow* over your very imperfect success, then that is quite enough to clear you of the charge of reigning hypocrisy.

The keeping of the heart is supremely important because "out of it are the issues of life"; it is the source and fountain of all vital actions and operations. The heart is the warehouse, the hand and tongue are but the shops; what is in *these comes* from *thence*—the heart contrives and the members execute. It is in the heart that the principles of the spiritual life are formed: "A good man out of the good treasure of his heart bringeth forth that which is good; and an evil man out of the evil treasure of his heart bringeth forth that which is evil" (Luke 6:45). Then let us diligently see to it that the heart be well stored with pious instruction, seeking to increase in grateful love, reverential fear, hatred of sin, and benevolence in all its exercises, that from within these holy springs may flow and fructify our whole conduct and conversation.

This work of keeping the heart is *the hardest of all.* "To shuffle over religious duties with a loose and heedless spirit will cost no great pains; but to set thyself before the Lord, and tie up thy loose and vain thoughts to a constant and serious attendance upon Him: this will cost something! To attain a facility and dexterity of language in prayer, and put thy meaning into apt and decent expressions, is easy; but to get thy heart broken for sin whilst thou art confessing it; be melted with free grace, whilst thou art blessing God for it; be really ashamed and humbled through the apprehensions of God's infinite holiness, and to *keep* thy heart in *this* frame, not only in, but after duty, will surely cost thee some groans and travailing pain of soul. To repress the outward acts of sin, and compose the external acts of thy life in a laudable and comely manner, is no great matter—even carnal persons by the force of common principles can do this; but to kill the root of corruption within, to set and keep up an holy government over thy thoughts, to have all things lie straight and orderly in the heart, this is *not* easy" (John Flavel).

Ah, dear reader, it is far, far easier to speak in the open air than to uproot pride from your soul. It calls for much less toil to go out and distribute tracts than it does to cast out of your mind unholy thoughts. One can speak to the unsaved much more readily than he can deny self, take up his cross daily, and follow Christ in the path of obedience. And one can teach a class in the Sunday school with far less trouble than he can teach himself how to strengthen his own spiritual graces. To keep the heart with all diligence calls for frequent examination of its frames and dispositions, the observing of its attitude toward God, and the prevailing directions of its affections; and that is something which no empty professor can be brought to do! Give liberally to religious enterprises he may, but give himself unto the searching, purifying, and keeping of his heart he will not.

This work of keeping the heart is *a constant one*. "The keeping of the heart is such a work as is never done till life be done: this labor and our life end together. It is with a Christian in this business, as it is with seamen that have sprung a leak at sea; if they tug not constantly at the pump, the water increases upon them, and will quickly sink them. It is in vain for them to say the work is hard, and we are weary; there is no time or condition in the life of a Christian, which will suffer an intermission of this work. It is in the keeping watch over our hearts, as it was in the keeping up of Moses' hands, while Israel and Amalek were fighting below (Exod. 17:12); no sooner do Moses' hands grow heavy and sink down, but Amalek prevails. You know it cost David and Peter many a sad day and night for intermitting the watch over their own hearts but a few minutes" (John Flavel).

27 Some Corollaries and Consequences of Keeping the Heart

Having sought to show that the keeping of the heart is the great work assigned the Christian, in which the very soul and life of true religion consists, and without the performance of which all other duties are unacceptable to God, let us now point out some of the corollaries and consequences which necessarily follow from this fact.

A. *The labors which many have taken in religion are lost.* Many great services have been performed, many wonderful works wrought by men, which have been utterly rejected by God, and shall receive no recognition in the day of rewards. Why? Because they took no pains to keep their hearts with God in those duties; this is the fatal rock upon which thousands of vain professors have wrecked to their eternal undoing—they were diligent about the externals of religion, but regardless of their hearts. How many hours have professors spent in hearing, reading, conferring, and praying, and yet as to the supreme task God has assigned have done nothing. Tell me, vain professor, when did you shed tears for the coldness, deadness, and worldliness of your heart; when did you spend five minutes in a serious effort to keep, purge, improve it? Think you that such an easy religion can save you? If so, we must *inverse* the words of Christ and say, "Wide is the gate and broad is the way that leadeth unto life, and many there be that go in thereat."

B. *If the keeping of the heart be the great work of the Christian, then how few real Christians there are in the world.* If everyone who has learned the dialect of Christianity and can talk like a Christian, if everyone who has natural gifts and abilities and who is helped by the common assisting presence of the Spirit to pray and teach like a Christian, if all who associate themselves with the people of God, contribute of their means to His cause, take delight in public ordinances, and pass as Christians were real ones, then the number of saints would be considerable. But, alas, to what a little flock do they shrink when measured by *this* rule: how few make conscience of keeping their hearts, watching their thoughts, judging their motives. Ah, there is no human applause to induce men to engage in this difficult work, and were hypocrites to do so they would quickly discover what they do not care to know. This heart work is left in the hands of a few hidden ones. Reader, are *you* one of them?

C. *Unless real Christians spend more time and pains about their hearts than they have done, they are never likely to grow in grace, be of much use to God, or be possessors of much comfort in this world.* You say, "But my heart seems so listless and dead." Do you wonder at it, when you keep it not in daily communion with Him who is the fountain of life? If your body had received no more concern and attention than your soul, what state would it now be in? Oh, my brother or sister, has not your zeal run in the wrong channels? God may be enjoyed even in the midst of earthly employments: "Enoch walked with God, and begat sons and daughters" (Gen. 5:19)—he did not retire into a monastery, nor is there any need for you to do so.

D. *It is high time the Christian reader set to this heart work in real earnest.* Do not you lament, "They made me the keeper of the vineyards; but mine own vineyard have I not kept" (Song of Sol. 1:16)? Then away with fruitless controversies and idle questions; away with empty names and vain shows; away with harsh censuring of others—turn upon yourself. You have been a stranger long enough to this work; you have trifled about the borders of religion too long: the world has deterred you from this vitally necessary work too long. Will you now resolve to look better after your heart? Haste you to your closet.

28 Some Advantages of Keeping the Heart

The heart of man is his worst part before it be regenerate, and his best part afterwards; it is the seat of principles and the source of actions. The eye of God is, and the eye of the Christian ought to be, principally fixed upon it. The great difficulty after conversion is to keep the heart with God. Herein lies the very pinch and stress of religion; here is that which makes the way to life a narrow way, and the gate of heaven a straight one. To afford some direction and help in this great work, these articles have been presented. We realize their many defects, yet trust that God will be pleased to use them. No other subjects can begin to compare with it in practical importance.

The general neglect of the heart is the root cause of the present sad state of Christendom; the remainder of this book might readily be devoted unto the verifying and amplifying of that statement. Instead, we merely point out briefly one or two of the more prominent features. Why is it that so many preachers have withheld from their congregations that which was, so obviously, most needed? Why have they "spoken smooth things" instead of wielding the sword of the Spirit? Because their own hearts were not right with God: *His* holy fear was not upon them. An "honest and good heart" (Luke 8:15) will cause a servant of Christ to preach what he sees to be the most essential and profitable truths of the Word, however displeasing they may be to many of his people. He will faithfully rebuke, exhort, admonish, correct, and instruct, whether his hearers like it or not.

Why have so many church members departed from the faith and given heed to seducing spirits? Why have multitudes been led away by the error of the wicked, turning the grace of God into lasciviousness? Why have so many others been attracted to companies of notional professors, which, despite their proud boasts of being the only people fathered together in (or unto) the name of Christ, are, for the most part, people who have only an acquaintance with the letter of Scripture and are strangers to practical godliness? Ah, the answer is not far to seek: it was because they had no *heart* acquaintance with the things of God. It is those who are sickly and diseased who fall easy victims unto the quacks; so it is those whose hearts are never rooted and grounded in the Truth who are tossed about with every wind of doctrine. The study and guarding of the heart is the best antidote against the infectious errors of the times. And this leads us to point out some of the *advantages* of keeping the heart.

A. *The pondering and garrisoning of the heart is a great help to the understanding in the deep things of God.* An honest and experienced heart is a wonderful aid to a weak head. Such a heart will serve as a commentary upon a great portion of the Scriptures. When such a one reads the Psalms of David or the Epistles of Paul, he will find there many of his own difficulties stated and solved: he will find them speaking the language of his own heart—recounting *his* experiences, expressing *his* sorrows and joys. By a close and regular study of the heart he will be far better fitted to understand the things of God than graceless rabbis and inexperienced doctors—not only will they be clearer, but far sweeter unto him. A man may discourse orthodoxly and profoundly of the nature and effects of faith, of the preciousness of Christ, and the sweetness of communion with God, who never felt the impressions or efficacy of them upon his own spirit. But how dull and dry will these notions be unto those who have *experienced them.*

Ah, my reader, experience is the great schoolmaster. Much in Job and Lamentations will seem dull and uninteresting until you have had deeper exercises of soul. The seventh chapter of Romans is not likely to appeal much to you until you make more conscience of indwelling sin. Many of the later psalms will appear too extravagant in their language until you enjoy closer and sweeter fellowship with God. But the more you endeavor to keep your heart and bring it into subjection unto God, to keep from it the evil solicitations of Satan, the more *suited to your own case* will you find many chapters of the Bible. It is not simply that you have to be in the "right mood" to appreciate, but that you have to pass through certain exercises of heart ere you can discover their appropriateness. Then it is that you will have "felt" and "tasted" for yourself the things of which the inspired writers treat. Then it is that you will have the key which unlocks many a verse that is fast closed unto masters of Hebrew and Greek.

B. *Care in keeping the heart supplies one of the best evidences of sincerity.* There is no external act which distinguishes the sound from the unsound professor, but before this trial no hypocrite can stand. It is true that when they think death to be very near many will cry out of the wickedness and fear of their hearts, but that signifies nothing more than does the howling of an animal when it is in distress. But if you are tender of your conscience, watchful of your thoughts, and careful each day of the workings and frames of your heart, this strongly argues the sincerity of it; for what but a real hatred of sin, what but a sense of the divine eye being upon you, could put anyone upon these secret duties which lie out of the observation of all creatures? If, then, it be such a desirable thing to have a fair testimony of your integrity, and to know of a truth that you fear God, then study, watch, keep the heart.

The true comfort of our souls depends much upon this, for he that is negligent in keeping his heart is generally a stranger to spiritual assurance and the sweet comforts flowing from it. God does not usually indulge lazy souls with inward peace, for He will not be the patron of any carelessness. He has united together our diligence and comfort, and they are greatly mistaken who suppose that the beautiful child of assurance can be born without soul pangs. Diligent self-examination is called for: first the looking into the Word and then the looking into our hearts to see how far they correspond. It is true the Holy Spirit indwells the Christian, but He cannot be discerned by His essence; it is His operations that manifest Him, and these are known by the graces he produces in the soul; and those can only be perceived by diligent search and honest scrutiny of the heart. It is in the heart that the Spirit works.

C. *Care in keeping the heart makes blessed and fruitful the means of grace and the discharge of our spiritual duties.* What precious communion we have with God when He is approached in a right frame of soul: then we may say with David, "My meditation of him shall be sweet" (Ps. 104:34). But when the heart be indisposed, full of the things of this life, then we miss the comfort and joy which should be ours. The sermons you hear and the articles you read (if by *God's* servants) will appear very different if you bring a *prepared* heart to them! If the heart be right you will not grow drowsy while hearing or reading of the riches of God's grace, the glories of Christ, the beauty of holiness, or the needs-be for a Scripturally ordered walk. It was because the heart was neglected that you got so little from attending to the means of grace!

The same holds good of prayer. What a difference there is between a deeply exercised and spiritually burdened heart pouring out itself before God in fervent supplication and the utterance of verbal petitions by rote! It is the difference between reality and formality. He who is diligent in heart work and perceives the state of his own soul is at no loss in knowing *what* to ask God for. So he who makes it a practice of walking with God, communing with God, meditating upon God, spontaneously worships Him in spirit and in truth: like David, he will say, "My heart is inditing a good matter" (Ps. 45:1). The Hebrew there is very suggestive: literally it is "my heart is boiling up a good matter"; it is a figurative expression, taken from a living spring, which is bubbling up fresh water. The formalist has to rack his mind and, as it were, laboriously pump up something to say unto God;

but he who makes conscience of heart work finds his soul like a bottle full of new wine—ready to burst, giving vent to sorrow or joy as his case may be.

D. *Diligence in keeping the heart will make the soul stable in the hour of temptation.* The care or neglect of the conscience largely determines our attitude toward and response unto solicitations of evil. The careless heart falls an easy prey to Satan. His main attacks are made on the heart, for if he gains *that* he gains all, for it commands the whole man! Alas, how easy a conquest is an *unguarded* heart; it is no more difficult for the devil to capture it than for a burglar to enter a house whose windows and doors are unfastened. It is the watchful heart that both discovers and suppresses the temptation before it comes in its full strength. It is much like a large stone rolling down a hill—it is easy to stop at first, but very difficult after it has gained full momentum. So, if we cherish the first vain imagination as it enters the mind, it will soon grow into a powerful lust which will not take a nay.

Acts are preceded by desires, and desires by thoughts. A sinful object first presents itself to the imagination, and unless *that* be nipped in the bud the affections will be stirred and enlisted. If the heart does not repel the evil imagination, if instead it dwells on it, encourages it, feeds on it, then it will not be long before the consent of the will is obtained. A very large and important part of heart work lies in observing its first motions, and checking sin *there*. The motions of sin are weakest at the first, and a little watchfulness and care then prevents much trouble and mischief later. But if the first movings of sin in the imagination be not observed and resisted, then the careless heart is quickly brought under the full power of temptation, and Satan is victorious.

E. *The diligent keeping of the heart is a great aid to the improving of our graces.* Grace never thrives in a careless soul, for the roots and habits of grace are planted in the heart, and the deeper they are radicated there the more thriving and flourishing grace is. In Ephesians 3:17, we read of being "rooted and grounded in love": love in the heart is the spring of every gracious word of the mouth and of every holy act of the hand. But is not *Christ* the "root" of the Christian's graces? Yes, the originating root, but grace is the derivative root, planted and nourished by Him, and according as *this* thrives under divine influences, so the fruits of grace are more healthy and vigorous. But in a heart which is not kept diligently those fructifying influences are choked. Just as in an uncared-for garden the weeds crowd out the flowers, so vain thoughts that are not disallowed, and lusts which are not mortified, devour the strength of the heart. "My soul shall be satisfied as with marrow and with fatness; and my mouth shall praise thee with joyful lips: *when* I remember thee upon my bed, and meditate on thee in the night watches" (Ps. 60:5-6).

F. *The diligent care of the heart makes Christian fellowship profitable and precious.* Why is it that when Christians meet together there are often sad jarrings and contentions? It is because of unmortified passions. Why is their conversation so frothy and worthless? It is because of the vanity and earthiness of their hearts. It is not difficult to discern by the actions and converse of Christians what frames their spirits are under. Take one whose mind is truly stayed upon God; how serious, heavenly, and edifying is his conversation: "The mouth of the righteous speaketh wisdom, and his tongue talketh of judgment: the law of his God *is in his heart*" (Ps. 37:30-31). If each of us was humbled every day before God under the evils of his own heart, we should be more pitiful and tender toward others (Gal. 6:1).

G. *A heart well kept fits us for any condition God may cast us into, or any service He has to use us in.* He who has learned to keep his heart lowly is fit for prosperity; and he who knows how to apply Scripture promises and supports is fit to pass through any adversity. So he who can deny the pride and selfishness of his heart is fit to be employed in any service for God. Such a man was Paul; he not only ministered to others, but looked well to his own vineyard (see I Cor. 9:27). And what an eminent instrument he was for God: he knew how to abound and how to suffer loss. Let the people defy him, it moved him not, except to indignation; let them stone him, he could bear it.

H. *By keeping our hearts diligently we should the soonest remove the scandals and stumbling blocks out of the way of the world.* How the worthy name of our Lord is blasphemed because of the wicked conduct of many who bear His name. What prejudice has been created against the gospel by the inconsistent lives of those who preach it. But if we keep *our* hearts, we shall not add to the scandals caused by the ways of loose professors. Nay, those with whom we come in contact will see that we "have been with Jesus." When the majestic beams of holiness shine from a heavenly walk, the world will be awed and respect will again be commanded by the followers of the Lamb.

Though the keeping of the heart entails such hard labor, do not such blessed gains supply a sufficient incentive to engage diligently in the same? Look over the eight special benefits we have named, and weigh them in a just balance; they are not trivial things. Then guard well your heart, and watch closely *its love for God.* Jacob served seven years for Rebekah, and they seemed unto him but a few days, for the love that he had unto her. The labor *of love* is always delightful. If God has your heart, the feet will run swiftly in the way of His commandments: duty will be a delight. Then let us earnestly pray, "So teach us to number our days, that we may apply our hearts unto wisdom" (Ps. 90:12)—as we "apply" our hands unto manual tasks.

Let me now close the whole of these chapters with a word or two of consolation to all serious Christians who have sought to give themselves faithfully and closely to this heart work, but who are groaning in secret over their apparent lack of success therein, and who are fearful that their experience falls short of a saving one. First, this argues that your heart *is* honest and upright. If you are mourning over heart conditions and sins, there is something no hypocrite does. Many a one is now in hell who had a better head than mine; many a one now in heaven complained of as bad a heart as thine.

Second, God would never leave you under so many heart burdens and troubles if He intended not your benefit thereby. You say, Lord, why do I go mourning, all the day having sorrow of heart? For long have I been exercised over its hardness, and not yet is it broken. Many years have I been struggling against vain thoughts, and still I am plagued by them. When shall I get a better heart? Ah, God would thereby show you what your heart by nature is, and have you take notice of how much you are beholden to free grace! So, too, He would keep you humble, and not let you fall in love with yourself!

Third, God will shortly put a blessed end to these cares, watchings, and heartaches. The time is coming when your heart shall be as you would have it, when you will be delivered from all fears and sorrows, and never again cry, "O my hard, vain, earthly, filthy heart." Then shall all darkness be purged from your understanding, all vanity from your affections, all guilt from your conscience, all perversity from your will. Then shall you be everlastingly, delightfully, ravishingly entertained and exercised upon the supreme goodness and infinite excellency of God. Soon shall break that morning without clouds, when all the shadows shall flee away; and then we "shall be *like him*, for we shall see him as he is" (I John 3:2). Hallelujah!